I JUST CAME TO SEE YOU

a MEMOIR

CHUL HYUN

I Just Came to See You: A Memoir
Published by Palisades Books
Palisades, NY

ISBN: 979-8-218-23377-8
BIOGRAPHY & AUTOBIOGRAPHY / Personal Memoirs

Artwork by Sarah Hyun. Copyright ©2023.

Cover and interior design by Victoria Wolf,
wolfdesignandmarketing.com, copyright owned by Chul S. Hyun.

The conversations in the book all come from the author's recollections,
though they are not written to represent word-for-word transcripts. Rather,
the author has retold them in a way that evokes the feeling and meaning
what was said and in all instances, the essence of the dialogue is accurate.

QUANTITY PURCHASES: Schools, companies, professional groups,
clubs, and other organizations may qualify for special terms when ordering
quantities of this title. For information, email chulhyunmd@gmail.com.

For my parents

CONTENTS

PROLOGUE

I HAVE WANTED TO WRITE this memoir for quite some time now. When I told a few folks, some responded, "What for? After all, it's just another memoir. Who will read it?" But writing this memoir allowed me meaningful moments to reflect on my life. Living in today's rapidly changing and demanding world, we have little time to stop and look back. We only look forward and keep moving ahead. Making an effort to pause can be worthwhile. In this writing process, I recaptured many past events, both sad and joyful, revealing their deeper meaning in my life. Writing this memoir has been an act of hugging myself and celebrating my life. I invite everyone to do it.

Another important reason for writing this book is to share my story with others, especially members of young generations born to immigrant families in the US. But then, how many of us are not children of immigrants in the US? This book is built on themes of immigration, culture, and identity, which are especially important today as people move around the world. Specifically, this book is my life journey as a Korean American physician, living with the influence of Asian and American cultures in the face of many challenges. I hope my pursuits of learning, improvement, self-esteem, and resilience linked to disparate stages of my life will be of interest and value to many who face challenges as they move from one country to another.

My experiences may show others how they can stay resilient in pursuing their dreams, as we all live in a competitive world full of bumps and unexpected challenges. As we undergo new experiences, our identities continue to evolve. However, it is vital to maintain our uniqueness and not change like a chameleon changes its color. We can adapt while retaining our original color, allowing us to create new perspectives.

The US is a composite nation of different ethnicities and cultures. It's like the Korean dish kimbap, which is cooked rice (bap), vegetables, fish, and meat rolled in seaweed (kim). In kimbap, the individual ingredients retain their original characteristics while collectively forming a new identity. Similarly, we must live in harmony, embracing others and respecting the cultures and values they bring to our society while still valuing our original cultures.

We all have unique stories to share. I hope readers from different backgrounds will connect with my stories and see how my experiences resonate with their own. By sharing our experiences, we can have moments to reflect on our past and present, leading us to cherish our lives, legacies, and futures.

My mother passed away eight years ago at ninety-two, and I remember her repeatedly saying during the last decade of her life, "There is a book I want to write—a collection of the thoughts I have gathered in my life. When your daughter grows up, I won't be around to tell her all these myself …" I still feel guilty for my laziness and indifference in not helping her write such a book. My mother-in-law, who passed away a few years after my mom, must have felt the same way about wanting to pass on her stories. All parents worldwide might feel the same way, especially those who immigrated to the US, wanting to pass on their legacies and heritages. I'm not sure what my mother specifically intended to write, but I hope my stories in this book reflect at least a small part of what she wanted to convey.

Writing this book took me on an insightful journey. I gained a clearer understanding of my present self by reflecting on my father's life and my own experiences. Looking back at these memories revealed unique perspectives about life. I realize that my family roots and the individuality I cherish are crucial in shaping who I am and how I live my life.

I.
UNEXPECTED
VISIT

IT WAS NOVEMBER 1976. Baltimore's weather had become chilly, and most of the leaves had fallen from the trees. I returned to my dormitory room after class and found a memo from George, my dorm-mate, left on my door.

"Chul, your dad is here at school. He is waiting for you in the lobby of Eisenhower Library."

Dad must have arrived at the Baltimore train station and called my dorm phone. I rushed to the library wondering, *Why did he come so suddenly with no notice?*

I have many memories of my dad, but his surprise visit to Johns Hopkins during my undergraduate senior year remains the most vivid. His visit on that chilly day still evokes my warmth and love and, ultimately, a longing for my dad, who passed away in 1995. I feel his absence profoundly, and while losing a loved one is something we must all accept, especially as we age, thinking of him makes me miss him deep down in my heart.

The year 1976 was a difficult time for my family. We were newly settled immigrants, so his visit was especially unexpected and alarming in my young mind. When I arrived at the library, I saw my dad sitting in the lobby. In his overcoat, a hat on his lap, he appeared lonely. Perhaps he was also stooping a little, feeling a touch out of place waiting for me.

I approached him, and his face lit up with a smile as he saw me. I hurriedly walked up to him and said, "Dad, this is such a surprise. How did you get here?" But, of course, I knew he would have taken a train from Penn Station in New York City to get to Baltimore.

I think the next question that came out of my mouth was, "Anything wrong?" meaning, "What are you doing here, Dad?" Why was I not friendlier to my dad? I could have been warmer and kinder. That's the least I could have done.

To my abrupt questions, Dad smiled and said, "Oh, everything is fine. I had the afternoon to myself and decided to visit you. I just wanted to see you."

He just came to see me?

Smiling, he asked, "Are you busy? Can we have lunch?"

I said, "Of course we can have lunch. How was your train ride?" We continued talking as we walked to a local Chinese restaurant near the campus.

"How is your study going?" he asked.

I replied, "I'm doing fine."

"Is your graduate school application going okay?" he asked again.

I replied, "Yes, Dad. I'll probably go to a school in upstate New York."

My dad had known by then that I wasn't applying to medical school that year. I told him over the summer that I was planning to pursue my PhD before applying to medical school. But I couldn't stop feeling awkward over lunch. I was sorry for not applying to medical school after my undergraduate work. I know my dad had hoped to see me become a doctor soon. And now I wasn't sure that would happen at all. I felt burdened and guilty because I had disappointed him. He seemed to understand my feelings and said nothing about it. But he was always like that—always overly understanding. In some way, I would have felt better if he had expressed his disappointment in me. Was he suppressing his true feelings?

We spent about an hour at the restaurant. "I just came to see you," Dad said again. Was it because of the chilly fall weather? He appeared melancholy and sad. We had been in the US for only a few years, but he looked tired. His face seemed to say, "I am fine as long as you are fine." I still remember how he appeared when he turned away to leave the campus. He looked lonesome and even depressed.

Kids today may not understand why this visit was such a big deal. It was the '70s, and we didn't have today's social media to communicate whenever we wanted. We had phones, cars, and highways, and various means of transportation, but they weren't as accessible and convenient as today. There was no Uber or Lyft. The usual methods of communication were letters and phones—not smartphones, but phones with cords and extra costs for long distance. People handwrote notes on paper, with no Microsoft Word on the computer with its autocorrect for spelling and grammatical errors. We would put the handwritten letters in an envelope, lick the postage stamp, and place it on the top right-hand corner of the envelope after writing out the sender and receiver addresses. Then came a quick trip to the mailbox, where we would drop it in. We would wait a week and sometimes more to receive letters. Waiting was not always bad. It allowed time to anticipate. It taught us patience.

So, for my dad to travel from New York to Baltimore on a random afternoon, unannounced, was a big deal. Also, to have him just share a meal with me and then travel back home on the same day was even more out of the ordinary. It was the last thing I expected.

My parents were living in Flushing, New York City. They had just moved to this big city that was fast-paced, diverse, and with frenetic energy like no other place. And they were stressed and anxious.

In Korea, my dad had a great job working as a trade expert for the Korean government. In 1973, he and my mother immigrated to the US. When they arrived, they initially settled in a Baltimore suburb. My father invested most of his money into a gift shop in a small strip mall. I still remember the name of the shop—Stacey's. But the business didn't do well, and he soon had to close the shop. They then moved to New York City to look for work. It was not easy for someone who had been well established in his own country to all of a sudden look for a job in a new country, challenged by a different language and social system. Also, my parents were not young. They were in their fifties.

After searching hard for several months, my dad was able to find a job handling accounts at a small company. Considering his previous job and the position he enjoyed, how *miserable* he must have felt working in this job. It wasn't until I was fifty that I wondered about this and imagined his hardship. How disappointed he must have been with his life. At the same time, I think he endured such hardships for my brother and me. In his mind, it was his duty and obligation.

In the US, it is common for immigrant parents to prioritize their children's education over their own careers and personal lives. This was true for my parents as well. My older brother and I were studying abroad at the time of my parents' immigration.

If my father had stayed in Korea, my brother and I would have had to return to Korea from studying abroad to serve in the army for three years. My father did not want our education to be interrupted in this way. So he chose to resign from the lofty job that he had worked so hard to get and took the uncertain path of moving to a new country. My parents were setting their feet on an immigrant's journey on an unknown path.

Why does his visit to Johns Hopkins stand out among so many memories of my dad? Why now, after so many years? It is not a mere longing for Dad. On the contrary, it creates a unique warmth and curiosity in my heart to seek a better understanding of my life. It leads me to travel down this path of memories.

II.
ROOTS

EVERYONE'S LIFE IS A MARATHON—some in severe weather, others with clear skies, but all with unique steps that take us in specific directions—and mine is no different. I was born in Seoul, Korea, and lived there until the age of fourteen when my family and I left to live abroad. (Unfortunately, Korea is divided now. When I write "Korea" in this book, I am referring to South Korea.) After finishing junior high school in Taiwan, I moved to Okinawa, Japan, and attended an international high school. After that, I came to the United States to attend Johns Hopkins University and other learning institutions. I became a physician and have practiced medicine for three decades. Growing up in different countries, I appreciated cultural diversity and its importance for a successful global society. Recently, I returned to school to study public health. Clearly, I am taking the approach of lifelong learning.

My journey has taken many twists and turns, and I've learned so much about how migrating to other countries shapes the culture and identity of immigrants, and how the insights they gain can enhance the ways they contribute to their new nations. I want to tell you all about that. But first, let me start with a little background about my roots.

MY PARENTS

My father, Philip Usup Hyun, was born in June 1919 in Korea and passed away in 1995 in New Haven, Connecticut. He was born in Cheongun-dong, Jongno-gu, a district in central Seoul. I never met my paternal grandfather, Yoon Hyun. My grandfather worked at the Industrial Bank of Korea, and my grandmother, Jungsik Kim, was a stay-at-home wife and mother. They had five boys and four girls; my father was the fourth son, and he was right in the middle. On big holidays such as New Year's Day, we would get together at the home of my "big uncle," as it was a tradition to get together as a family in the eldest son's house on major holidays. There were thirty-plus children, so there was always deafening chatter and lots of fun.

My father graduated from Whimoon High School and went to the Business School of Yonsei University in Seoul. After graduation, he went to Japan for graduate school and returned to Korea in 1945, when Korea became free from Japan's colonial rule.

Beginning in middle school, he played ice hockey, and by the time he was in college, he was the ice hockey team captain. During college, my dad traveled to play ice hockey in Hwanghae-do (located in North Korea now) and Hokkaido, Japan.

Based on what I've heard from his sisters and friends, my father was trendy. He was popular among his guy friends and the ladies in nearby universities. Growing up, I often heard my aunts saying, "Chulsoo-ya (a familiar form of referring to someone younger), you have no idea how popular your dad was as a college student."

I would ask, "How do you mean?"

Then my aunts would say, "When your dad hopped into the jeon-cha (an old version of an electric streetcar operated on rails) with skates on his shoulder and a hockey stick in his hand, college girls would go crazy. They wouldn't stop staring at him."

Ever since I was little, my dad would take me to ice hockey games between Yonsei University and Korea University. I learned to skate from my dad's playful yet serious lessons and skated throughout my childhood. He enjoyed skating until he passed away at seventy-six. People loved to watch him as an elderly gentleman gliding with such grace.

I have distinct memories of my dad watching many comedies on Japanese TV. I didn't find these shows interesting, but my father was practically glued to them. So one day, I asked him, "Why do you like comedies so much?"

He replied, "I find them relaxing. It's an escape where I can find myself doing anything I wouldn't normally be able to do."

My mom told me, "Did you know he wanted to attend drama school?"

I was shocked because my father was relatively quiet. He wasn't an introvert, but he wasn't an extrovert either.

I asked, "Did he want to become an actor?"

Mom smiled and replied, "Well, believe it or not, yes!"

However, when he applied to Yonsei University, the school he wanted, the theater department was on break. So he majored in business instead. I sometimes think if my dad went to theater school and became an actor, I would now be a second-generation actor.

My dad was always gentle and rarely got upset over anything. A true gentleman, he was generous to his friends and others who needed help. He taught me and my brother, Chulkyu, by example, taking a calm and considerate approach to life. He listened to his sons and accepted us for who we are. I have a long way to go to be like him.

When Chulkyu and I misbehaved, we were punished by going to the corner of the room and holding up our hands in the air. Dad would scold us, "You boys should be ashamed of yourselves. Go to the corner and raise your hands!"

Chulkyu and I would find a space in the corner, kneel, and raise our hands. There was a large mirror in front of us, reflecting our images. We would look at each other and start giggling. I was able to see my dad through the mirror's reflection, and I would catch my dad trying not to break out laughing. He would say, "What's going on? Do you boys find this funny?"

My brother and I would say out loud in unison, "No, sir!"

But Dad always felt sorry for us. So we never had our hands up for more than ten minutes.

He would always come by early and ask, "Will you do it again or what?"

My brother and I immediately would say, "No, sir. We will not misbehave again!"

That would be the end of our punishment.

Where my dad was forgiving, my mom was the opposite. Unlike my dad, who could not endure any punishment for us, my mom meted out her sentences with no qualms. For example, she would punish us on summer vacation for not doing our homework.

She would practically beat us with a broom. No kidding. She would wield the broom just like a police officer would wield a club.

Chulkyu and I had to find a way to avoid seeing her when we returned home late at night. Chulkyu would say, "Chulsoo-ya, go in first if you like. But I won't. It is not safe now. Mom is not sleeping yet."

I would typically reply, "Yeah, but it's already past eleven. I will go in and deal with it." My brother strategically came home late at night to be safe from Mom's wrath, but I was not as bright.

My mother's maiden name was Kyungbae Kim. She was born in September 1923 in Gongju, Chungcheongnam-do, Korea. She graduated from Seoul Girls' High School and went to Japan to study at Tokyo Women's University. After college, she went to Manchuria as a high school teacher and later worked for the YWCA in Seoul and the Korean Ministry of Commerce. She met my father there and married him in 1949. She had one younger sister.

My mother excelled in all aspects of academic and extracurricular activities. She was invited to live in the school founder's home—an honor extended to only one or two top students in her class. She was also an outstanding tennis player and competed in representing her school. My mother was atypical of women of her generation. It was when very few women went to university for advanced study. Yet she chose to go abroad to Tokyo to attend a university. She was courageous, outspoken, and dauntless in the face of the unbelievable challenges of that era. During the early 1940s, while she was a schoolteacher in Manchuria, she actively participated in the Korean independence movement. She was also a social activist promoting social reforms, especially for women. As an active member of YWCA, she led campaigns supporting the rights of working women and their active participation in all aspects of life and politics. She was very social and a natural leader.

My mother was also a fantastic cook. Growing up, I remember her dedication to making excellent food for our family. Her naengmyeon (cold noodles) and mandoo (dumplings) were matchless. I have fond memories of her delicious dishes that pop up whenever I smell the scents of Korean food.

Like many romantic relationships, my parents had ups and downs and, thankfully, no severe pitfalls. They shared a common goal to raise their children healthy and well educated. Moving to the US forced them to sacrifice for their children's interests, creating unexpected hardships for them to endure. Despite the challenges they faced, they supported each other and remained strong and resilient. They were married for forty-six years until Dad passed away. I remember Mom's loving care for Dad as he was going through chemotherapy in his last two years.

Mom had a more assertive personality than Dad, which made most of the quarrels go her way, and Dad would concede. The most significant conflict I remember was over Dad's smoking habit. Dad was a heavy smoker, quickly consuming three packs of cigarettes a day until his early forties. One day, they argued over smoking, after which Dad left home. He didn't come home for the next three days. When he finally returned home, he never smoked again. He was a man of strong will.

My maternal grandfather's name was Hyunseung Kim, and my maternal grandmother's name was Booksoon Kim. My maternal grandfather was born in Gongju, Chungcheongnam-do. After graduating from high school in Korea, he went to Keio University in Japan to study law. He returned to Korea in 1923 and worked for his people in the field of law. I never met him.

Around 1965 when I was in elementary school, I went to Gongju for a memorial service for my maternal grandfather, and so many people came to join us. There, I met my uncle, Mr. Kim, the principal of

Gongju High School. He was also the most well-known horticulturist for chrysanthemums. Following the memorial service, we visited Uncle Kim's home and enjoyed an exceptional Korean meal.

My uncle would say, "I haven't seen you boys for a long time. Let me guess what you would like to eat for dinner." He knew exactly what we wanted to eat. My brother and I still remember our aunt's kimchi jjigae (stew), which consisted of only kimchi and some pork. It is still one of the most delicious dishes I have ever had.

After his postgraduate study, my father tried working in several different businesses with little success. In 1961, our family moved to Chungju, Chungcheongbuk-do for my father's new job at the Chungju Fertilization Plant. He worked there for a year as one of the directors before we all moved back to Seoul, where he took a new job as a founding member of the Korea Trade Promotion Corporation (KOTRA) in 1962.

When we lived in Chungju, I was in first grade. Chungju was a rural country town, and with little else to do, my brother and I played army games with our friends. In the winter, we enjoyed sleigh riding and skating. The school I attended was a typical rural school. The kids did not have backpacks, so they would wrap their books in cloth and tie them around their waists. My brother and I were among the very few students who had backpacks. I felt terrible being one of the few kids with a backpack, so I wrapped my books like my friends and tied them around my waist. My mom found that out and scolded me for doing that. Many students could barely afford lunch, which is hard to believe by today's standards. The school gave out cornbread to students from low-income families. My mom would make me hot lunches and deliver them daily, and I used to ask her to bring me a lot more to share with my friends.

When I was in second grade, we returned to Seoul. First, we lived in Anam-dong, and then we moved to Suyu-ri. My brother and I attended Donam Elementary School. I was busy with after-school programs, but whenever I had a little time, I loved to play cards and marble games with my friends. By the time I was in third grade, I had started learning judo, and my dad enrolled me at a judo school in Sogong-dong. He told me, "If you want to learn something, you should go to the 'real' place," and he sent me to Judo University, the largest judo training center in Seoul. I was the youngest in the school.

My first day of judo school was January 17, and it also happened to be minus seventeen degrees Celsius outside! The room had no heating, and I was freezing. I remember one instructor yelling, "If you are cold, run!" So I have never forgotten that January 17 when it was minus seventeen degrees. Both running and martial arts (judo and tae kwon do) played crucial roles throughout my life. Besides the physical benefits, the mental empowerment, such as self-control and focus, was enormous. This helped me deal with stress and anxiety in daily life. It allowed me to develop a stable mindset and persevere through challenges.

DAD'S ROLE IN KOREA'S ECONOMIC DEVELOPMENT

In the '60s, Korea was still an impoverished country. The Korean War ended in 1953 as the country went into a truce. Peace came, but the economic conditions of the country were miserable. In 1960, we would see many beggars and homeless orphans on any street, with plain clothes on their backs, skeletal frames, and hungry eyes. The orphans wandered the streets carrying empty cans. I can still remember that fishy smell from the cans.

This made me feel very sad. I often ran into them at the gate when they waited outside until the housemaid went to the kitchen to fetch some leftover food. One time, a group of beggars came knocking at the gate. When I opened the door, I saw one of them who was about my age. He wore old, shabby clothes, and his face was stained with specks of dirt from not washing his face in a while. He looked at me and around at our home, carefully observing what I was wearing, and said, "Do you have any cooked rice?"

"Yes, she will get you some. Please wait," I promptly replied, feeling sorry about the huge contrast between our situations.

At the beginning of 1960, very few people had televisions. There were only three bridges crossing the Han River, and nobody would ever have dreamed about Gangnam (now a famous district in Seoul). The Korean government was busy trying to rebuild the economy. Trade was essential at the time for a country like Korea with minimal natural resources.

KOTRA, where my dad worked, was a quasi-governmental organization whose sole purpose was to promote trade and related businesses internationally. KOTRA played a crucial role in creating a miracle economy in Korea. In 1965, KOTRA founded a trade academy, which specialized in international trade. My father was the first principal of this academy. In later years, my father would go abroad to build more KOTRA branches in major cities in Asia. Recently I was thinking about my dad, and I went to the KOTRA website. I found a picture of him taken in 1965 when the trade school celebrated its opening. My heart raced with pride and joy at seeing this picture.

When I was in the fourth grade in 1964, Korea participated in the World Trade Expo for the first time. It was an epic event for my country and its economy. I remember my dad being especially busy preparing for this event. My dad's primary job was to create a strategy to raise awareness of Korean products and their brands among industry experts and to forge new business relationships with consumers world-wide. The year 1964 was when Korea hit a hundred-million-dollar trade goal for the first time. But so much has changed since then. Korea has experienced one of the most significant economic transformations since the '60s. With a GDP of $1.64 trillion in 2020, Korea is now the tenth-largest world economy. It is now the world's major electronics, telecommunication equipment, and motor vehicle producer. How did this industrialization miracle take place? One primary reason for this success story is Korea's export-led growth strategy, building a network of free trade agreements with numerous countries, and my dad was a part of that.

DISTANT BROTHERS

My brother, Chulkyu, is two years older than me. We are extremely different. I am often too idealistic and naïve, taking my time to reason and sort things out slowly. I like things around me to be close to perfect, if not perfect. And I am a dreamer. On the other hand, my brother is practical, realistic, and spontaneous.

Though we were two years apart, he went to school one year early, so we were three grades apart. My brother is witty and a quick thinker. He has a good sense of humor. In contrast, I'm a bit slower. I think and ponder outcomes before I speak. My brother used to tease me and call me a "fluorescent lamp" because fluorescent lights back then did not turn on instantly. Instead, they would flicker a few times before they lit up. My father would defend me by saying, "But a fluorescent light is still faster than a television." The television screens back then took their sweet time to come to life.

Chulkyu was amiable and, unlike me, had a lot of friends grow-ing up. I was relatively quiet and shy. My brother had no problem approaching new people and becoming their friends in a short time. And he was popular among girls. He went to Whimoon Middle School, my dad's alma mater, and he joined the Boy Scouts there. I remember he was on the cover of *Hagwon* magazine, which was extremely popular among teenagers in the '60s.

Sitting at dinner as a teenager, I would get upset over certain social injustices in the news, whereas my brother seemed relatively unbothered by these things. He would say, "Yeah, but that's the way it is, you know. Those with more political or financial power get to do more things." Obviously, he knew far more than I did then.

In contrast to me, my brother was efficient. He was far more realistic than I was. He was also fashionable and cared about his looks and clothes from early on. Chulkyu behaved more maturely and dated girls older than his age. In high school, he dated college students. In college, he dated ladies working jobs. I asked him, "Why do you always date older girls?"

He said, "The girls at my age are not for me. They are too young, and I can't even find common things to discuss with them. But, on the other hand, older girls are more mature, and they are more fun to go out with."

Pondering these differences, I sometimes wondered if we were indeed related. Chulkyu was supposed to be the closest person to me, but I never knew him well enough. The last time we enjoyed each other's company was probably during elementary school in Chungju when we played military games with other kids. When he entered middle school, I was in fourth grade. From then on, we took different paths. Since we left Korea, our paths diverged even further. My brother went to Madrid, Spain, to study, and I came to the US to attend college. Now I live in the US, and he lives in Korea. Despite all these differences between my brother and me, I still miss him. Now that we are both over sixty years old, our interactions all became beautiful memories.

III.
FIRST
STEPS
ABROAD

OKINAWA: FIRST ENCOUNTER WITH OTHER CULTURES

To discuss my life abroad, I must begin with my junior high and high school days. After graduating from elementary school in 1967 in Seoul, I left for Okinawa. My father had a new job at the Korea Trade Office branch in Okinawa, and our family followed him.

In Okinawa, my father dealt with businesses and government agencies, playing intermediary roles between Korea and Okinawa to facilitate successful trade negotiations. To prepare for these negotiations, he had to be familiar with and learn the current economic situation in both countries and research how these negotiations could eventually promote the Korean economy. He was a trade strategist.

Okinawa is surrounded by the East China Sea and the Pacific Ocean, south of Japan, and is the largest of fifty-five Ryukyu Islands. It is a vacation island where an American military base is located. The beautiful corals in Okinawa's transparent, emerald ocean water are unforgettable.

Although Okinawa is now part of Japan, it has a culture, language, and history of its own separate from those of Japan. My father hired a tutor for my brother and me to learn the Japanese language, but I complained that I wasn't ready for another foreign language, not even being able to speak English well enough at that point. Now I have regrets about not taking full advantage of those tutors since my Japanese is subpar.

Ryukyu Kingdom, a small tributary state of Imperial China, played a central role in the maritime networks of medieval East Asia and Southeast Asia, having active trade relationships with Japan,

China, Korea, and other Asian countries. Japan eventually annexed the Ryukyu Kingdom in 1879 to form Okinawa Prefecture.

My first trip to Okinawa was via Osaka, Japan. I stayed for two days in Osaka and took a plane to Okinawa. I remember visiting several places in Osaka, and one of them was Osaka Castle. Toyotomi Hideyoshi, a Japanese samurai who launched an invasion of Korea in 1592 that failed and ended with his death, had governed the Osaka Castle.

Even though I was young, I was familiar with the long-standing, bitter history between Japan and Korea. What I had learned from history books and newspapers gave me a negative impression of Japan. One of my hobbies during elementary school was making scrapbooks out of exciting articles. I remember collecting many articles on history, especially about Japan and Korea. Despite being close neighbors, Korea and Japan have had a testy and often hostile relationship. There were many reasons for such hostility between these two countries, including hundreds of invasions by the Japanese since the tenth century, which culminated with a complete annexation of Korea by imperial Japan in 1910. That lasted until 1945 when Japan surrendered.

Understanding the historical significance of these facts made me prejudiced toward Japan. I had negative images of Japan and the Japanese people. Of course, these are not without good reason, but as I recollect right now, I find it amazing that I had these impressions at such an early age. Maybe that is why the Japanese language and people got on my nerves when I arrived in Osaka. I knew Okinawa would differ from Japan, but I was curious how different it would be. *How am I going to live there? I need to make friends,* I worried to myself.

When I arrived in Okinawa, it was February. In contrast to the cold weather in Seoul, the weather in Okinawa was nice and warm. Before we arrived, I could look down from the plane at the beautiful emerald waters. As soon as I landed, I remember eating so many bananas and oranges that I was running to the bathroom numerous times afterward. Bananas and oranges were rare in Seoul then, and realizing how abundant they were in Okinawa, I was delighted and began to think that living in Okinawa would not be so bad.

My dad worked in Naha, the capital of Okinawa. We first lived in a foreigners' village half an hour away from Naha. We then moved to the inner city of Naha. Both American civilians and military personnel mainly occupied the village we lived in near Naha. There was a supermarket, and I remember it carried, in addition to all sorts of groceries, ice cream in various flavors. I immediately became a regular customer.

There are many beautiful places in Okinawa. The shimmering, jade-colored water sparkles in the sunlight, and the ocean-side drives provide fantastic views. Driving along the Pacific Ocean, the highway was so close to the sea that it felt like the waves were touching the bottom of our car. On weekends, my family used to go out driving, and I remember going to the A&W drive-in at the top of the hill. From there, we would have the most fantastic vista overlooking the Pacific Ocean and beyond. Still, to this day, I don't think I have ever had more delicious cheeseburgers and milkshakes than I had there.

The scenic views from the ocean-side highway in Okinawa were vastly different from the small alleyways and narrow streets of Seoul that I knew. The vastness of the ocean made me breathe more deeply and freely. The island is two-thirds the size of Jeju, the largest island in Korea, and it is long, spanning a three-hour drive from north to south. But it takes only a half hour to reach the ocean from anywhere on the island. I loved snorkeling and swimming in the sea and often went snorkeling with friends, diving down three to five meters to look at the corrals and floating among beautiful tropical fish.

CHRIST THE KING SCHOOL

During the late '60s, there were three American schools in Okinawa: Okinawa Christian School, Christ the King School, and Kubasaki American School. Initially, I enrolled at Okinawa Christian School to learn English. Subsequently, I enrolled in Christ the King School, a Catholic international school belonging to the School Sisters of Notre Dame. The principal was a nun, but most teachers were non-clergy civilians. Students were diverse, with different ethnic and racial backgrounds. They were predominantly Filipinos, Caucasian Americans, Japanese, and biracial among these groups.

Students wore uniforms. The boys wore white shirts and a tie with an embroidered school logo, beige pants, and maroon-colored jackets, and the girls wore similar-colored skirts and jackets. Like most teenagers, the boys wanted to look cool, so they loosened their neckties, and the girls would try to hike up their skirts. Then, when the nuns were near, the girls would pull their skirts back down to make them longer.

The school included grades from kindergarten to twelfth, but each class was small. Classmates had a great collegial relationship. Despite the strict environment, we still had a lot of freedom. While most of the students were Catholic, a few, like me, were not. Many of the school's basic principles were associated with Catholicism, such as strong moral values, personal integrity, and compassion for others. Students made their own independent choices, regardless of what others may think. My teachers were excellent, and students had academic freedom to express their independent views. The school valued an individualized scholarship approach, creating space for individual interests and meaningful collaboration among students. Some teachers took part in developing extracurricular activities such as plays and independent studies with students. I remember Mr. Sicam, my physics teacher, spending many extra hours outside class hours to tutor me. The school provided an exceptional learning environment that inspired me to become a lifelong student.

JAPAN'S REVERENCE FOR ARTISANS

I had the opportunity to meet an elderly Korean master potter, a descendant of the Yi Dynasty (1392–1910), who lived two hours north of Naha in a city called Nago. A reporter from a Korean news outlet flew to Okinawa to interview this potter, and I followed the reporter and his crew. In the interview, I learned that the master potter's ancestors were taken prisoner by the Japanese after the war between Japan and Korea four hundred years ago. I wondered how the potters then might have overcome the struggles for their survival.

This master potter was a soft-spoken man with a courteous manner. As we all sat on his tatami mat, he knelt, prepared tea, and served us gracefully. During the interview, he told the crew that his ancestors settled in Okinawa about two hundred years ago. There were many other Korean potters living throughout Okinawa. *Wow, that's amazing that the descendants of Korean potters are living as potters in Okinawa,* I thought to myself.

Around the fourteenth century, Korea, Japan, and China were the major countries in Asia that produced high-quality pottery. However, Korean potters were regarded as lower-middle-class people then. In contrast, potters were highly respected in Japan and belonged to a higher class. Because Japan treated potters with respect, this helped promote further technology, art, and culture associated with pottery in that country. I've heard some Koreans claim that others are exploiting the artistry created by Korean potters. However, I find that to be unreasonable. Creation is essential, but perhaps even more important is supporting the development and industrialization of these crafts, as they undoubtedly shape culture. Japan did this successfully.

RESCUE AT NAHA PORT

In the summer of 1969, my mom woke me up early in the morning, "Chulsoo-ya, wake up! Dad needs your help! It's urgent."

A small fishing vessel from a little southern sea town in Korea near Yeosu encountered a hurricane and drifted six hundred miles down to Okinawa. There were about ten fishermen in the boat who fought to stay alive during this storm. My brother and I hurriedly carried Mom's food to these fishermen at the dock at Naha Port. They had been fishing in the southern sea of Korea and battled a storm for a week. Finally, they drifted toward Okinawa and were found and rescued by the US Navy.

When I arrived at the dock, I saw that the men looked worn down and tired. Their skin was scorched and dried from the sun and saltwater. As I entered the lower portion of their boat, I saw a man about fifty years old. I asked him, "Are you okay? Do you need more water?"

He weakly smiled and replied, "Yes, please." It appeared he had little energy even to speak. The men looked awful. I felt sad looking at them. *They must be fathers to people like my brother and me*, I thought.

I looked at the ill-equipped boat. *How could this boat have survived the hurricane?* I wondered. This incident happened when Korea was still very poor, with a GDP per capita of less than three hundred dollars. For comparison, the US GDP per capita was five thousand dollars back then. Poverty and lack of resources were the reasons these men were out on this boat, chasing fish to feed their families.

I handed out the food and drinks my mom prepared, and we took these men to hotels where they could wash up, rest, and sleep. I was busy until the next day. When things like this happen today, the Korean embassy or the consulate will step in. But at the time, there were no entities like that representing the Korean government other than my father's office. The Korean consulate office was established in Okinawa three years after this incident.

MULTICULTURAL IMMERSION IN TAIWAN

My family lived in Okinawa for two years. In 1970, my father went to Taipei, Taiwan, to open a new trade office, so our family followed him. At the time, Taiwan was known as the Republic of China, and its president Chiang Kai-shek claimed to be the sole legitimate representative of China. Mainland China, or the People's Republic of China, was under the rule of Mao Zedong.

I attended Taipei American School in Shilin, a suburb of Taipei, Taiwan. The school taught in English, and its curriculum was similar to that of US schools. But once we stepped outside the school, it was a different country; we were essentially in China. Taipei American School was one of the largest international schools, with students from more than forty countries. Not having lived abroad for long, I regarded this school environment as a human zoo, where I was one of the species. I met and interacted with students from the US, China, Japan, Europe, Africa, and other countries. I learned so much from my diverse classmates. As I got to know them as friends, my curiosity about their cultures and histories was piqued. I saw how cultures and histories were distinct and unique for each of us.

Like Korea, Taiwan also was invaded and colonized by Japan. In 1895, China's Qing Dynasty lost the Sino-Japanese War, and as a result, Taiwan was occupied by Japan until 1945 when World War II ended. After Chinese communists took control of China in 1949, President Chiang Kai-shek and his supporters fled to Taiwan.

SPEAKING WITH CONFIDENCE

In Taipei, few people understood English, so I enrolled in a Chinese language class at Taiwan University and started to learn Chinese. Living in a foreign country always presents issues with language and many memorable interactions. One day, I went to Taipei's open market to buy some fruit. Since my command of the language wasn't good, I pointed at the oranges and said in my imperfect Chinese, "Give me four of those, please."

The Chinese lady at the fruit store looked at me, surprised, and asked, "Shei sile?"

I couldn't understand her and was puzzled. Finally, an elderly lady beside her explained to me in Japanese that the woman had asked, "Who died?" Later I found out that, in Chinese, the word for the number four and the word death are pronounced quite similarly but with different intonations. I did finally succeed in buying four oranges, but this embarrassing episode is still vivid in my mind.

Another time, I wanted to go to the zoo, so I hopped in a taxi. I realized I forgot to check how to say zoo in Chinese, but it was too late since I was already in the taxi. The driver asked me, "Chi nali?" which means "Where to?" I hesitated, and he asked me again, "Chi nali?" more loudly and this time less politely.

I was embarrassed but decided to say, "Chi dong wu yuan," because in Korean, the zoo is dong-mul-won, and Chinese is sometimes similar to Korean since many words share the same characters.

But unfortunately, the driver didn't understand. He asked me again, more irritated this time, "Chi nali?"

His voice had escalated, and I didn't appreciate it. I decided to be very confident and repeated myself, almost feigning intonation, and said, "Chi dong wu yuan!"

The taxi driver understood this time and drove me to the zoo. I thought, *Ah, when you speak a foreign language, you must speak confidently!*

KOREA'S LOST TREASURES

In our first year in Taipei, we lived in Daan District, which was close to National Taiwan University. The next year, we moved to Shilin, where my school was located. The nearby Taiwan National Palace Museum featured all kinds of art and cultural artifacts spanning five thousand years of China's history, including more than six hundred thousand amazing drawings, sculptures, and treasures.

When I thought about Korean history, which is older than five thousand years, I wondered, *What can we show the world?* Japan and China have invaded Korea nearly a thousand times, and almost all of our national treasures and artifacts have been stolen or lost. There are a few items in the Korean section of the New York Metropolitan Museum of Art, but unfortunately, they don't fully showcase Korea's rich history and culture. How can we restore all these lost and forgotten treasures of our ancestors? With our physical remnants of past treasures buried and gone, how can we share the story of Korean history and culture with others?

SPARRING OVER HISTORY

One memory that stands out from my life in Taiwan involves all the quarrels I had with my Chinese friends about the history of Korea and China. Many of my Chinese friends mistakenly thought Korea was part of China. Given the geographic proximity and numerous interactions and conflicts between the two countries over several millennia, the confusion may be understandable to some extent. But make no mistake—the two countries are distinct. Korea originated in today's northeastern part of China and Manchuria, making these areas once the homeland of ancient Korea. Therefore, the origins of each kingdom, the dynasties of both countries, and their histories are distinct. The languages of Korea and China also are different. Korean is phonetic with an alphabet, in which one pronounces a word the way it is written. In contrast, Chinese is tonal, using characters.

There is a saying that if you live in a foreign country, you become a patriot. I had a friend, John Li, whose father owned banks in Hong Kong. A kid from a wealthy family, John was the same age as me. He had moved to Taipei from Hong Kong, and we were in the same math class. We often went to the cafeteria during lunch hours and had many discussions. Unfortunately, our viewpoints often collided when we began discussing the histories and relationship between Korea and China. Our meetings invariably turned into quarrels and would last *more* than a few days. You would find me running to the library to read up on the ancient history of Korea to prepare for my anticipated quarrels with John Li. Many of these arguments concerned territorial issues between Korea and China over centuries.

One day, I said, "John, do you know about the Goguryeo Dynasty, which covered Manchuria, the eastern part of today's China?"

John replied, "That's not possible. Manchuria has always belonged to China, and Goguryeo was a part of China. I learned that from my history books."

I was upset at his reply but calmed myself. "Oh, no, John! You're not informed correctly. Goguryeo was one of Korea's ancient dynasties from the first century to 668 AD. It was a powerful kingdom that survived invasions of the Han and Sui dynasties."

John paused, not quite knowing what to say next.

So I added, "I'll give you proof that Manchuria was Goguryeo's territory. The tombstone of King Gwanggaeto the Great of Goguryeo is in Jian, in the Jilin Province of China."

This tombstone (shown in the drawing below) is one of the major primary sources for determining the history of Goguryeo. It supplies invaluable historical detail on Gwanggaeto's reign and insights into Goguryeo and its adversarial relationship with China.

Our arguments went on and on, and although we never got physical, we came close sometimes. Reflecting on these memories, I see now that these were expressions of our adolescent love for our respective countries, which brings a smile to my face. We naturally look at other countries' histories and cultures through our own lenses. My experiences with John and other friends from China and Japan helped me learn not to be too judgmental of one country over another.

BACK TO OKINAWA

I started high school in Taipei but returned to Okinawa to finish at Christ the King School. Besides American students, there were students from more than ten countries. My study strategy was simply to concentrate on my classes and do my best. I had difficulties with my English, but at the same time, it was an exciting challenge.

Having studied in an English-speaking school for only a few years by then, I wasn't proficient in English, which played a crucial role in all my studies. Motivation and attitude mattered a great deal. I tried to think in English, but it wasn't easy. Aside from different grammar and other linguistic structures between Korean and English, cultural differences and associated body language also mattered. For instance, while direct eye contact with elders can be considered rude in Korea, it was necessary for communication in the Western world. It took a while for me to get used to this.

I clearly remember meeting Mr. Johnson, the principal of Okinawa Christian School, during the first week I arrived in Okinawa. I was about to enroll at the school to learn English. Mr. Johnson was a tall man, probably about six feet five. With a bit of English, I knew I had to introduce myself. "Hello, Mr. Johnson. How do you do? My name is Chulsoo Hyun." I spoke barely above a whisper, initially making eye contact. But soon, I felt it was not polite to continue maintaining eye contact with him.

In another example, we tend to be more formal in Korean culture when conversing with older individuals. But I realized that formality could be a sign of stiffness. On the other hand, a lack of formality could lessen professionalism.

My high school days were when I experienced the first and most significant tension in my life. I worked twice as hard as my classmates to keep up. Those of you who have experienced adjusting to foreign languages and cultures will understand. I remember practically memorizing pages of my American History textbook. Since I was not fluent in English, I was not a fan of essay questions. When answering those questions, I wrote down the responses I had memorized from the textbook. The teacher initially suspected I was cheating. But then she found out later that I had memorized the whole page. It was extremely time-consuming, and I could have been more effective in preparing for tests.

Typically, the best way to answer essay questions is to understand and describe the material in your own words. While I understood the material, my English was not good enough to explain what I knew in my own words. So I chose a more laborious way—memorizing the entire page. I remembered an old Korean saying, "If you have no teeth, you use your gums to eat." This was the only way I could achieve my goal of getting a perfect score on tests. I knew I had to persevere in adapting to a new method. But how?

One thing that helped me build discipline and resilience was running. I remember vividly when I started running regularly in high school. It was hot most of the time in Okinawa. Running out on the road was an exhausting but exhilarating experience.

Academic rigor and interests were intense, which were even more important to survive and succeed. But I had to build strength, both mental and physical, to be able to sustain my goal. So I ran. I remember running under that scorching sun of Okinawa against traffic on the road, and running made me focus my energy and sort through challenges. I dreamed of becoming a successful person: a scientist, physician, linguist, historian? These were all my interests, and I kept telling myself that I needed to work harder than most of my friends. I felt I just had to. So I went out to run, and it was my way of refreshing my mind and body to be ready for the next day. Running was my way of building discipline and resilience. It helped me keep my motivation and not give up on my pursuits.

I know many other ways to relax. My friends and I went to beaches to swim and listen to music, but running was the best for me. And it was running that taught me how to tune and control my life. Running has ups and downs, and one must distribute an adequate amount of energy to avoid getting fatigued too early or developing cramps. Running also helped me learn how to persevere and endure. It required discipline, and it helped me thrive and survive.

COLLEGE APPLICATIONS

The graduating students in my class applied to universities throughout the world, but most of them applied to colleges in the US. I also applied to schools in the US, but I considered universities in Munich, Heidelberg, and London. However, I decided it would be best for my long-term goals to pursue an education in America.

I ended up coming to the US as an international student with an I-20 Visa. I-20 is required for international students to enroll at certified colleges and universities in the US. Like today, college applications included high school GPA, SAT score, a personal essay, and recommendation letters. When selecting a college, I considered what I wanted to major in. However, my thinking was limited. It was nerve-racking to apply, and I looked at schools based on information provided by college brochures, which was all I had to rely on. I had no campus tours and no internet then. Neither did I have access to the school's alumni to learn from. There were uncertainties. But I felt there was enough information for me to choose a school. I believed that as long as I worked hard, I would do fine regardless of where I went.

I found Johns Hopkins University very appealing among the many schools I looked at. It was neither small nor large, and it would be perfect for settling in. No matter what I wanted to major in, it was a school with more than enough resources, so I felt confident in my decision to go there. Hopkins had only eighteen hundred undergraduates with about four hundred fifty per graduating class, which seemed like an adequate size. The number of graduate students mirrored the number of undergraduates, so I thought it was also a perfect setting for research.

HIGH SCHOOL GRADUATION: CHALLENGE AND TRIUMPH

In my senior year, I was the captain of the track team and the chairperson of the National Honor Society. I also participated in the scholastic bowl team. Every day after class, I took part in one of these activities for two to three hours, and when I came home, it was time for dinner.

Because of my limited English, my SAT verbal score was low, but I had a higher TOEFL verbal score. The Test of English as a Foreign Language (TOEFL) was offered to international students. Luckily, I was able to graduate as valedictorian. I still remember how I found out. Three months before graduation, at lunchtime, my homeroom teacher Mrs. Kolpack called me in, along with Cora and Koumei, two of my classmates. We looked at each other, wondering what this could be about. Because Mrs. Kolpack called me along with two of the top students in our class, I felt somewhat relieved, thinking it couldn't be a bad thing. Cora and Koumei were probably thinking the same.

As we walked toward Mrs. Kolpack's desk, Koumei asked, "Hey, guys, do you know why she is calling us here?" We all looked at each other quizzically, and Cora replied, smiling as always, "No, I don't."

As we sat around Mrs. Kolpack's desk, she congratulated us first and said that one of us was the valedictorian and the others were the salutatorians. Koumei and I looked at Cora with envy and admiration because Cora had always been the top student and we figured she had to be the valedictorian. Our teacher sensed this and shook her head gently, saying, "Chulsoo, you are the valedictorian." It was an unbelievable moment!

I remember staying up several nights preparing my speech. I was beyond nervous at the thought of having to give an address before a large audience. This inevitability resulted in many sleepless nights filled with stress and anxiety. I titled my speech "Rebirth." My opening sentence went like this: "As a caterpillar goes through the process of metamorphosis, we, the graduates, are also in one of the most important cycles in our lives …"

One of the school's traditions was that before the graduates' procession, students enter with flags of their respective countries. According to my mother, the Korean flag came first since I was the valedictorian. She would always share this story proudly with all her friends. Honestly, I don't remember, and I don't think that the Korean flag came in first, but I didn't want to deny my mother's proud moment.

Maybe this was one of the ways I fulfilled my filial duties as her son. I went to Johns Hopkins, and Koumei went to MIT. Cora went to Cedar Crest with a full scholarship.

Years later, I attended my high school reunion in 2001 in Las Vegas. It was exceptional to see my former prom date, Mariko, and many of my other classmates again after twenty-eight years. I still hear news about my classmates and teachers from the Christ the King School website, managed by Cora. While some information is good, other news, especially about the deaths of classmates and teachers, makes me sad. I was also disappointed to find out that the school closed in 1989. There is now a Japanese Catholic school at the exact location.

IV.
HIGHER
ED
JOURNEY

FRESHMAN YEAR AT JOHNS HOPKINS UNIVERSITY

Room 302 on the third floor of Jennings Hall was my first home in the United States, the dormitory room I was assigned at Johns Hopkins in August 1973. The freshman dormitory buildings were located around the Freshman Quad and cafeteria. It was this quad where some of my classmates hung a mannequin of a General Chemistry professor during my freshman year. General Chemistry was the very first course all the premeds had to take. Once, a professor gave a difficult test that many students failed. As revenge, students hung a dummy in his image on the quad grounds. Later the class apologized.

I remember a public phone visible straight ahead as you entered Jennings Hall. There were bathrooms on the second floor. My room was on the left side of the hallway as one walked up to the third floor. There was no internet nor cell phones then, and that public phone in the corner of the first floor was the only direct means of communication with others far away. I wonder if that phone is still there, or is it gone like many old relics of the years?

Many years later, when my daughter Sarah was about ten years old, I took her to Johns Hopkins Homewood Campus, and then we all revisited Hopkins on a campus trip in 2014 when she was applying to colleges. All those buildings from the '70s remained. My old haunts of the post office, snack bar, and cafeteria were unchanged. I wanted to show her my old dormitory room, so I tried to enter Jennings Hall, but the school had locked the door, and we could not enter without a key.

During the '70s, it was uncommon to see many international students at Hopkins or any other US university. There were fewer than ten Asian students in my graduating class. When I visited Hopkins forty years later in 2014, however, I noticed many Asian American students on campus. I heard Korean being spoken by students in various areas, and there was a marked increase in the representation of all racial and ethnic groups. It is crucial for the entire campus community to embrace and engage with diverse identities, perspectives, and learning experiences in today's world. I was pleased to see that Hopkins was actively doing so.

My roommate, Bill, had come from Annapolis, Maryland. Bill's father was a history professor at the Naval Academy, and Bill told me he wanted to study history like his father. I thought Johns Hopkins was famous for science and medicine only, but the school had reputable departments in political science, history, and other humanities. Bill grew up in a Catholic family, and like me, he graduated from a Catholic high school.

While many students were rowdy in the dormitory, Bill and I were quiet. Bill had a gentle and scholarly demeanor. He woke up every morning at six and went to bed at ten. He was calm and prudent, and we lived peacefully in the same room. Some friends complained about their roommates, but I had no issues with Bill. When there was a lot of noise in the dorm that lasted for hours at night, Bill would smilingly say, "Hey, Chul, do you want to join me in the library?" So we escaped to a quiet place.

WHAT DO I WANT TO BE WHEN I GROW UP?

I had wondered many times in high school what I wanted to study in college. I have always had a deep interest in languages, having lived in places like Taiwan, Japan, and Korea. Different languages and cultures have always fascinated me. Language is an essential tool in understanding a country's culture. How languages are spoken—their similarities, differences, and origins—are deeply rooted in culture and history. I also liked math and physics. No matter how much I studied English, it was hard to get an A, but the more time I invested in math and physics, the more I could reap excellent results. It was also rewarding and enjoyable to receive recognition from my classmates and teachers in these areas.

I don't recall any advice I received about a major before applying to colleges. Of course, I wanted to pursue what I liked or excelled in. But, truthfully, now that I ponder this after many years, it seems that I sought what I thought I did best, not what I liked the most. And I question whether, even if the results are not as good, one should try to pursue what one wants to do most. But I was somehow unable to do that. I enjoyed instant gratification and recognition. Perhaps, I needed it badly then. At any rate, despite all my interest and passion for languages, I ended up studying natural sciences.

Pursuing natural sciences, I needed to figure out what I was getting myself into. I fancied becoming a scientist, researching, and making discoveries. Although my parents never pushed me to specialize in anything in particular, I knew they wanted me to go into medicine. Yes, my dad told me I should do whatever I liked and what made me happy. But when I told them I was interested in medicine, their eyes sparkled. They could not hide the thrill of their son possibly becoming a doctor. In retrospect, however, I felt compelled to focus on the areas where I could rapidly excel. Seeing my parents in a difficult situation as immigrants, financially and socially, I couldn't be relaxed about my choice. And no matter what my parents said to me, I felt an internal pressure to succeed in what I was doing.

At any rate, my parents did not restrict me, and my brother and I did what we wanted. For example, in 1968, my brother told my parents he wanted to go to Switzerland to study hospitality and become a hotelier. His proposal was rather shocking. However, despite his surprise, my father still managed to smile. Was that because he trusted his son? My father was gentle and generous; I don't think I inherited these characteristics. Thankfully, I inherited my mother's persistence and aggressiveness, which helped me commit to my goals.

AMERICA'S FIRST RESEARCH UNIVERSITY

"Research university" is the most used phrase to describe Johns Hopkins University. The founders modeled the school as a research-oriented university. The Hopkins mission has always been to research and seek new knowledge. Teaching and research go hand in hand. Such was the educational philosophy responsible for making today's Johns Hopkins University.

FIERCE ACADEMIC LIFE

As a nineteen-year-old college student, I was independent, away from my family, and proud. I was also very excited to meet hundreds of classmates. In my first year, in addition to chemistry, math, and physics,

I took a writing seminar, economics, and Spanish.

You cannot talk about Hopkins without mentioning premeds (premedical students). The first course for premeds was General Chemistry, and on the first day there were three hundred students in the class out of four hundred twenty in my entire class. All the students looked at each other smiling and relaxed, but deep down, we were competitors, and we could feel it in the air.

I was curious to think how many of these students would become my true friends with whom I could have open conversations. After one semester, the number of students in the General Chemistry class decreased by half; after a year, it dropped to one hundred. As the years passed, I would hear, "My test scores did not come out as expected. Maybe medicine is not for me." It went on this way so that by the senior year, about eighty students applied to medical school.

Premeds were very passionate about their studies. Students were in lecture halls, libraries, and dorms, besides spending time in the cafeteria for meals. Eisenhower Library closed at midnight, so many students went to Gilman Hall's reading room, which was open twenty-four hours a day. While some students were excessively competitive in their studies, there were generally more collaborative behaviors.

The fact that I graduated from high school as a valedictorian wasn't impressive in this environment. Out of the thirty-two people living in Jennings Hall, seven of us were valedictorians. At Hopkins, it was not possible for students to receive a high grade solely by studying the material covered in class, despite their best efforts. We had to understand the material and apply what we learned. Students used to call Organic Chemistry the "premed bible," so we worked hard to absorb everything we were taught in that class. In the lab, our job was to isolate unknown compounds and purify and quantitate them.

While doing these experiments, some students wouldn't even go to the bathroom because of the *intense* competition. I am not familiar with how competitive students were in the liberal arts. My roommate, Bill, and his friends put in a lot of effort, but it seemed like they were working in a more relaxed environment. In retrospect, I regret not having enough time to read books that weren't directly related to my coursework. Nevertheless, everything I went through at Hopkins, both failures and successes, served as a foundation for my future academic journey that continues to this day.

DETOUR TO COLUMBIA

While I was a freshman living in my dorm, my parents lived in a suburban Baltimore apartment. They wanted to live close to me, and they invested just about all their life savings into a gift shop located in a small shopping center in a Baltimore suburb. Their goal was to have a stable life and a consistent income. But it wasn't that easy. The gift shop did not work out, and they had to close the shop within six months.

My parents filed for green cards in Baltimore and had to wait for their permanent resident visas, which ended up taking some time. The year 1973 was economically and politically unstable in the US. There was the Watergate scandal in 1972, which stirred up political friction in the country. In addition, there was an energy crisis due to the war between the Arabs and Israel. As petroleum prices rose, the disruptions caused even more difficulties with my parents' immigration process in the US.

My parents thought that a larger city would be better for finding a job, so in 1974 they moved to New York City. They were unsure of their next steps, including what type of job to pursue and where to find opportunities. For them, the move was a leap of faith. I felt sorry for my parents, who had to navigate this new life. In the midst of all this, I thought that maybe if I transferred to a school in New York, I could spend time with my parents and help them out in any way I could. Unfortunately, my parents were not only economically challenged but also faced language barriers. My father spoke enough English to get by in Korea and Japan, but his English wasn't sufficient in the US.

Without telling my parents, I applied to transfer to Columbia University. If I had let them know I was doing this, they would have been against it. I figured I would get the results of my application within three months and would let them know in time. My main reason for the transfer was for my parents, but I was also curious to explore New York and be exposed to the bigger world. Because my life at Hopkins was mostly on campus, I had limited opportunities to experience the world beyond the school.

I met with the dean of Hopkins to explain my reasons for transferring. I told him I wanted to help my parents, who recently moved to New York City. Thankfully, I received an acceptance from Columbia University in February 1974.

When I broke the news to my parents, they were agitated, saying they didn't want to inconvenience me or interrupt my education. I told them, "I want to transfer to Columbia University. It's a big city, and I will have a lot more to see and learn."

They looked shocked. Dad said, "What do you mean? Is there any problem with your school now?"

"Oh, no. No problem at all. I am doing well at Hopkins. But you know Columbia is another reputable and even bigger school. It would be great to study in New York City."

Mom joined in. "Is that because we are moving to New York? We will be just fine. You don't need to worry about us."

I quickly replied, "No, of course it's not that, Mom. I want to study at Columbia. Then, I may be able to have more opportunities."

Mom persisted, "The last thing we want is to interrupt your study."

Trying to reassure them, I smiled and said, "Of course not. That won't happen."

My parents reluctantly accepted my assurances.

NEW YORK CITY TOUR GUIDE

I finished my first year at Johns Hopkins in May 1974 and went to New York to live with my parents. They lived in Greenpoint, Brooklyn. I remember it was very close to the Williamsburg Bridge. Since they had already lived abroad for the past seven years, they were adjusting to this new city life pretty well, except for financial difficulties. My dad found a job in a small office near Fifty-Seventh Street and Broadway in Manhattan, and my mom stayed at home. Compared to their previous life in Korea, I thought their new life was miserable, but they were thankful that they could manage to live in a new city.

During my first summer break in college, I took a job at a Japanese company. It was a travel agency owned by a second-generation Japanese American. It also had a large gift shop. Because I could speak some Japanese, I worked both at the gift shop and the travel agency. There were many Japanese people in the '70s traveling around the world. One of my duties was to go out to JFK Airport with a driver, pick up Japanese tourists, bring them to their hotels, and help them check in. I was also a guide taking tourists to many sightseeing destinations. This work allowed me to learn about New York City. In my remaining hours, I worked in the gift shop selling popular gift items, including watches and jewelry. I had no idea that my limited Japanese skills would come in handy in the US. Thanks to this job, I was able to earn good money while also exploring the city.

VASTLY DIFFERENT LEARNING ENVIRONMENTS

My first classes at Columbia started the week after Labor Day. Its campus differs greatly from the campus of Johns Hopkins, and Columbia has many more students. Columbia has traffic, people, and businesses on the Upper West Side of bustling Manhattan. In contrast, Johns Hopkins is on an idyllic campus with vines growing on red brick academic buildings in a park-like environment. At Columbia, I took political science, English, and history in addition to science classes. I wanted to delve into the humanities as well. I commuted from Brooklyn and made three subway transfers from Greenpoint to Union Square to Times Square and finally to 116th Street. It took about an hour to get to school. I did all my studying at the university library and on the train. There are many libraries on campus, but I avoided the large ones like Butler because it took so much time to go in and out. My favorite libraries were the ones at Kent Hall, the engineering building, and a small one in the math building near Broadway.

I usually left the library a little after 11:00 p.m. to take the train home. When I got bored reading my book, I would look around at the people on the train. I noticed that, starting from the Times Square stop, many people would hop on after their evening shifts. The people on the train were all different and varied depending on the sections of town. For example, on the train from Union Square to Brooklyn, there were many immigrants from Eastern Europe. The train was full of people speaking Russian, Polish, Czech, and many other languages. These commuters were heading back to their homes after a long and tiring day at work. They appeared exhausted.

Ah, that lady probably came from Europe. I wonder what country and how many kids she has? I thought. They may have kids like me going to college.

I spent my time trying to read their faces and minds. They were probably thinking about their homeland, and many of them looked worried. Their tired looks and facial expressions hinted at the challenges of their lives as immigrants. They could be my parents.

K-TOWN

There were very few Koreans in New York City in 1974, which was long before Koreatown was created. But on Broadway between Twenty-Eighth and Thirty-Fourth, which is now part of Koreatown, there were many signs such as "Kim's Wigs." There were only two Korean restaurants and one Asian grocery store. On the street, if you saw another Asian person, you would immediately look at each other with recognition and a knowing glance.

There are so many Korean churches nowadays, but back then there were only two in Manhattan. One of them was called Manhattan Korean Methodist Church. It was located right across from Columbia University on 115th Street. Korean American leaders built the church in 1921, commemorating the Korean national independence movement that began on March 1, 1919. Unlike many churches built by immigrants, this church was unique because most members were students who came to study abroad. Many students were political activists who dreamed of Korean independence from Japan.

Patriots passed through Manhattan Korean Methodist Church, resulting in a deep sense of Korean history there. Therefore, it was significant for me to attend this church. I imagined those young students with patriotic fervor because they had lost their country to

Japan and came abroad to study, all the while hoping for the liberation of their homeland. I am sure this church gave them hope and unity. Through faith in God, they felt independence for Korea was possible. This church also provided a way for later Korean immigrants to keep their identity and history while practicing their religion and adapting to new surroundings. Attending this church was a true blessing. My parents and I registered at the church, and I was baptized there in 1974.

In the late '70s, Koreans started immigrating in larger numbers, with the most significant influx in the '90s. Korean churches played a vital role in Korean American communities. Currently, there are more than two hundred Korean churches in the New York City metro area. Churches provide not only worship services but also weekly activities such as music programs for kids, programs for the elderly, and various educational services for newly arrived immigrants. Korean churches were also a place where people could make business connections, get employment, obtain housing, and, most importantly, provide a much-needed social connection among Korean people. Churches provided a haven where newly immigrated Koreans felt they were understood.

Toward the end of my second year at Columbia, I decided to return to Johns Hopkins. I realized that natural sciences were my area of interest, and I missed the friendly, homey, and quiet environment where I could concentrate on my studies. I wrote a letter to Dean Susskind, sending along my transcripts from Columbia, asking if I could return. He replied with a welcoming yes.

BACK TO JOHNS HOPKINS

My parents settled in Flushing, New York, and I returned to Baltimore in August 1975. I felt fortunate that I had the chance to study and live in the city. However, after spending fifteen months with my parents in a small apartment, I needed to be independent and wanted alone time.

Compared to New York City, Baltimore is a small city. Downtown Baltimore was not very safe back then, however. The Inner Harbor and other current city attractions did not exist in 1975. It was the perfect setting for being stuck in the library and studying. So I said to myself, *Now I must concentrate and study seriously.* I found a small studio apartment on Guilford Avenue three blocks away from campus, moved in, and got to work.

KINDRED SPIRITS

There was so much ruthless competition at Hopkins. I don't think I reached that level of compulsiveness or competitiveness, but at the same time, I don't know what my friends thought of me. Perhaps they thought I was overly ambitious. I liked studying at night. I woke up relatively late, often missing breakfast, and sometimes hurried to lectures at nine in the morning.

Many students were like me, but some of them had completely different lifestyles and study schedules. Let me introduce two friends of mine: Noah and Robert. Although they are actual people, I have changed their names.

Noah was premed and born in Sweden but grew up partly in the United Kingdom, graduating from high school in London. He came to the US to study. He and I shared similarities in that we both went to high school outside the US and came here as international students. Because of this, we could identify with each other, and we became good friends. Noah was tall and blonde, so he was easily recognizable. Even if it was raining or snowing, he always wore clogs. When he walked down the corridor of Gilman Hall's reading room, the sound of his clogs clacking was distinctive. Even from a distance, we could hear him walking to the library. Noah used to come to the reading room after midnight with a large cup of black coffee, grinning and saying, "How are you guys doing?" with a thick Swedish accent.

We often studied until five in the morning and fell asleep on a long sofa in the middle of the reading room in Gilman Hall. Then, at six in the morning, the woman who cleaned the hall would wake us up with her vacuum cleaner. She was a character. She would kick the sofa where Noah was sleeping. Then, to my sleeping friend and me, she would say, "Get up! This ain't no hotel!"

Noah and I would wake up, rubbing our eyes to those words and her noisy vacuum. We would then walk to the cafeteria for breakfast. Noah eventually became a neurosurgeon, currently practicing in the Midwest.

Another student was quite different from Noah. I will call him Robert. He was a third-generation Chinese American who came from the West Coast. He studied physics and tended to be reserved and introverted. I remember that only a small number of students in our class majored in physics, and he was one of them. From his sophomore year on, Robert lived off campus and did most of his work in his room. He would mainly go to lectures and the library, and then return to his apartment. His daily meal schedule was something like breakfast at six, lunch at noon, and dinner at six, eating all his meals in his apartment. He never drank coffee or ate junk food. He would go to bed at ten, and regardless of whether he had a term paper due the following day, he would always keep his schedule.

Friends would ask, "Hey, Robert, do you want to join us in Rathskeller?" (Rathskeller was a student bar on campus.)

Robert would reply, "No, thanks!" and walk away.

After a while, we stopped asking him. I don't think Robert had a lot of friends, but he always appeared to be content. His lifestyle was uniquely inspiring, but it was an outlier from the Hopkins standard at the time. He graduated at the top of our class. Because we are in different fields, I don't know what he's doing right now, but I hear from other friends that after finishing his engineering PhD he went to work at NASA.

SHARING MY CULTURE THROUGH TAE KWON DO

People say the college years are a time to explore life and discover who you are. It is also a time to make plans for your life. Besides obtaining knowledge through academic endeavors, we also try to find happiness and learn to get along with others in our society. My college life differed greatly from this kind of ideal. I was always running out of time, and time passed so quickly that I hardly had time to reflect on my life.

I needed a way to exercise, reduce my stress, and have a creative outlet. I went out to run occasionally but didn't engage in long runs like I used to do during high school. Instead, I restarted tae kwon do. It was an excellent way to be physically and mentally fit, which I had learned as a teenager in Taipei, Taiwan. My instructors had been masters dispatched by the Korean government to teach this unarmed martial art to the Chinese army in Taiwan. I eventually earned my black belt.

I thought it would be a great idea to start a club on campus, which I did in my third year. I motivated my friends, sent out a survey, and it turned out that a good number of students were interested in joining. My friends and I advertised through fliers and posters. I rented a wrestling room in the school gymnasium on Mondays, Wednesdays, and Fridays. I held classes those days from 7:00 to 8:00 p.m. and charged students forty dollars per semester.

Initially, twenty students attended, but after two months I had forty people in my club—to be exact, forty students and two faculty members. I remember one history professor, Dr. Kea, who joined. At the end of each semester, I invited a tae kwon do master from New York City, and we held a promotional test. Once a year, I also gave a demonstration. I continued my club activities until I graduated.

Because tae kwon do was Korea's traditional martial art, the club activity helped me connect with my ethnic identity. In addition to the income and health benefits, it encouraged me to express my Korean identity in an environment with few Asians. Teaching tae kwon do also improved my leadership skills. Unlike running, which I would have done alone or alongside a group of friends, tae kwon do required more group interaction. It offered me a challenge to meet and get along with new people. But most importantly, it filled me with joy.

GRATITUDE TO AMERICA

When I first started college, my dad gave me $2,500. Tuition at a private university was about $1,500 per semester, totaling $3,000 annually. Room and board were approximately $1,500 a year. So I needed $4,500 per year to attend college. In contrast, the tuition for private universities such as Johns Hopkins in 2023 is about $60,500. The total cost including room and board amounts to about $79,500. Since 1973, school tuition has increased more than twenty times. Even considering inflation during the past fifty years, where $4,500 in 1973 is worth about $31,600 in 2023, clearly college tuition has soared higher than the inflation rate.

Mr. Johnson was the director of financial aid at Johns Hopkins. In the second semester of my first year, he asked me, "You're still waiting for your permanent visa?"

Getting a loan as an international student was practically impossible. But since I applied for permanent residency (a green card), both the school and I assumed that I would be getting it soon so I would be able to apply for loans in my second semester. Mr. Johnson made this very clear. But I did not have my green card by the end of the first semester, making it impossible to apply for a loan. I told him I didn't have my green card but instead had a letter from my lawyer saying I had applied for one. So I asked Mr. Johnson, "Can you use this letter as proof for the impending permanent visa? I have no money."

For a moment, he looked contemplative. Then, he went over my documents and the letter from my lawyer and said, "Okay, let me try."

Fortunately, I could cover my tuition, room, and board half by loans and half by scholarship. I did the same thing during my second year at Columbia. I also had some money from summer jobs, but they were not enough to cover my tuition.

When I returned to Hopkins in my third year, I had to go through the same ordeal with Mr. Johnson. Again, he asked when I was getting my permanent visa. I could not answer. When physicians or nurses apply for permanent residency, they get it quickly. But for other professionals, the immigration process takes a long time. For this reason, I visited my lawyer's office several times, but all he could say was to be patient and wait.

How would anyone have known I would graduate from college and still not have a green card? Thanks to good grades, half of my tuition was covered by scholarships, but the other half was a big problem. Every semester I had to see Mr. Johnson, have the same conversation about my visa, and then ask for another loan. Was I too selfish?

I went to see Mr. Johnson just before the start of my fourth year's second semester. I was dragging my feet to the financial aid office. That I still did not have my green card was ridiculous. I agonized over how I could face him, wondering what excuse I would give this time. I felt so sorry to put him in the same difficult position over and over. But I was firm on my goal. I had to graduate somehow.

As I opened the door, Mr. Johnson noticed my hesitancy and spoke first. He said, "Hmm, no green card yet, huh?" He looked as if he had given up on me. "Well, you have only one semester left. Congratulations! Like the past semesters, we will try to cover half your tuition with scholarships and the other half with loans."

I was so thankful! As an international student, I felt privileged to be educated in the United States through scholarships and loans. Johns Hopkins owed me nothing but bestowed on me all these gifts. I felt like I needed to find a way to give back to my new country through my career.

DISAPPOINTMENT AND DELAY

As a premed since my first year, I had intended to apply to medical school in my fourth year. But two factors went against my plan. First, I was an international student still without a permanent visa. Second, getting into medical school as an international student was possible only if you had extremely high grades. Unfortunately, my grades were not good enough to put me in a competitive position for medical school. The fact that I could not apply to medical school immediately made me sad and depressed. I thought, *Maybe I was too arrogant and didn't try hard enough.*

Nevertheless, I did not want to give up. I couldn't afford to stay disappointed in myself for too long and had to make an alternative plan. I thought to myself, *I am still very young. There must be another way to go to medical school! Alright, I'll get my PhD in natural sciences and then apply to medical school.* Was I trying to make an excuse for myself? No, I was serious about that. I always wanted to become a medical scientist, so even if I went to medical school right after college, I would eventually try to get my PhD.

Furthermore, I would have a green card by the time I finished graduate school, making me more competitive. *So what if I get my PhD first and an MD later?* I consoled myself. *It is a long journey to medical school. It will prepare me to be stronger for the future. Life is long, and the next several years will be a tiny part of my life, anyway.* I had to accept this new grave situation and move quickly with a new plan. So I took the GRE and applied to the biophysics PhD programs that my professors recommended.

PURSUING A BIOPHYSICS PHD AT ROCHESTER

After graduating from Johns Hopkins, I attended the University of Rochester School of Medicine and Dentistry in the Department of Biophysics as a PhD candidate. Rochester is an interesting city located in the northwest region of New York State and is the third-largest city in the state. I thought it was a great place to live and raise a family, especially with its excellent public education system that ranks Rochester as one of the top education cities in the US. Although it snows a lot and gets pretty cold in the wintertime, the weather is milder in the spring and summer.

The University of Rochester is a private university founded in 1850. As a school with a strong emphasis on basic research, it shares many similarities with schools like Johns Hopkins and the University of Chicago. The University of Rochester is also famous for its George Eastman School of Music, named after the founder of Eastman Kodak.

In 1925, with help from George Eastman and John D. Rockefeller, the University of Rochester opened its medical school. The university's

School of Medicine and Dentistry is a product of a new era of medical education in the US. Until the early 1900s, most physicians had never undergone formal medical education. Medical education and hospitals in the US were woefully inadequate until the early twentieth century. They did not have proper laboratory and clinical facilities. Schools had no established teaching and curriculum standards, and hospitals lacked administration tools to run the hospitals. To control and regulate the medical activities of physicians, schools and hospitals had to create more systematic protocols, which called for more research. The University of Rochester's new medical school was among a handful of schools that revolutionized how medicine was taught across the country.

In the late '70s, there were relatively few students of diverse ethnic heritages in American universities. The University of Rochester was not an exception. Undergraduate students of Asian heritage were mostly children of immigrants, and many graduate students came abroad from India, Korea, and China. I was older than the undergraduate students but younger than the graduate students. Having left Korea at a young age, I was happy to meet Korean graduate students who became like older brothers to me. My Korean, which had become clumsy because of lack of use, significantly improved as I hung out with them. I also learned more about Korean culture and history.

In my biophysics PhD program, four other students came from different schools and specialties: a physics major from Cornell, a math major from the University of Maryland, a chemistry major from Harvard, and a biology major from a small college I had never heard of. I thought the last student was the smartest of them all. I learned from my previous experiences that a university's reputation does not always reflect its students' capabilities. I received an NIH predoctoral fellowship, which covered my entire tuition and a monthly stipend. I lived in the Graduate Living Center and paid minimal rent, which allowed me to live comfortably. Again, I was grateful. I would have been happy with just my tuition, so the stipend was a true gift.

PHD DISSERTATION ON CHOLERA TOXIN

I did research in biophysics laboratories during my junior and senior years at Johns Hopkins. Because of this background, I started my PhD research in the laboratory of Dr. George Kimmich, a world-renowned expert in the field of cell membrane transport. He was incredibly patient and understanding. Dr. Kimmich played a pivotal role in helping me engage with basic science research.

My specific topic of interest was cholera toxin. When cholera attacks people, a toxic protein (cholera toxin) secreted by the organism called Vibrio cholera generates acute diarrhea, resulting in severe dehydration. If patients don't receive treatment right away, they can die. While cholera is rare in developed countries, it is still endemic in numerous developing countries, with millions of cases yearly.

Cholera toxin causes an increase in the cellular level of cyclic AMP, which is a chemical mediator that interferes with electrolyte transport. My objective was to find the mechanism of altered electrolyte transport. I used the chicken intestine as a cell model. Experiments and required technical skills were demanding. I would stay in the lab many nights, often pondering what went wrong with my experiments. My experiments were often tedious, and many wouldn't work. If there is one strategy I learned from my graduate work, it was to remain patient and persistent. Good things take time.

Thankfully, I was productive and was able to finish my thesis within five years. After that, I went to the University of Chicago to continue my postdoc education. I chose Chicago because it was the home of a world expert in cholera toxin and electrolyte transport, Dr. Michael Field.

V.
BUILDING
CAREER AND
FAMILY

MIKI, APPLE OF MY EYE

In the fall of 1978, I met my future wife at the University of Rochester, a freshman from Long Island, New York. When we first met, she said, "Hello, my name is Mikyong, and I'm in my first year!" She approached me with a bright smile, and I was struck by her pretty, oval-shaped face and big eyes.

She was nineteen, and I was twenty-four. We attended the same church and started seeing each other often. That same year, after Thanksgiving break, I was studying alone at the Carson Library in Hutchison Hall. Miki had returned to campus from visiting home, and she approached me, smiling. She was holding a luscious-looking apple and offered it to me, saying, "Hi! This apple tastes great. Do you want it?" Of course, I accepted the apple eagerly, and without hesitation, I took a bite. Maybe if I hadn't, things would have turned out differently.

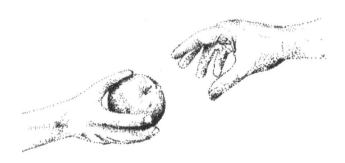

Mikyong (Miki) is one of three children in a family that immigrated from Seoul to the US in 1972. She has a brother two years older than her and a sister five years younger. When we met, her parents owned a dry-cleaning business in Long Island. They were devoted

Christians and worked hard for their children. Maybe because she was the oldest daughter, she looked more mature than me, even though I was five years older than her. When she shared stories about her family, it was clear to me that she took good care of her siblings and parents. Seeing her surrounded by her family was heartwarming, and I couldn't help but feel a twinge of envy. Our home environments were quite different. I missed the chance to enjoy the close bonds that were apparent in her family dynamics.

Did I mention that Miki has beautiful eyes? She is a natural beauty. When she smiles, it just makes me forget about everything. What drew me to Miki the most was her honesty and transparency. There was no pretense or makeup. She meant what she said, and her face showed it. She wasn't afraid to share her values and goals in life with me, and I agreed with many of her values. We had many commonalities. Miki also made me feel secure and comfortable.

Miki and I varied our date locations among the school libraries, coffee shops, parks around the city, and more. While studying, we often got hungry and went to the Wegmans supermarket. When we got tired of studying, we would go to Pittsford's Mendon Pond Park and take walks on its beautiful bird song trails. Letchworth State Park and Niagara Falls were our popular driving destinations. After dating for two years, in the summer of 1982, we took a drive to Niagara Falls.

One of our favorite locations was a park on the Canadian side, where we could have a full view of the American Falls. No matter how often we looked at the falls, they were always breathtaking. We could hear the burbling sound of falls. There were few people around us. It was a hot and sunny afternoon, but the breeze made us feel perfectly comfortable. We were standing, leaning toward each other, looking at the falls.

"Let's get married," I stated matter-of-factly.

It seemed to come out of nowhere, but it wasn't unexpected. We had known each other for four years and dated the last two. Knowing each other well, now was the time to think about our future seriously.

"You *are* the right person for me," I continued. "You bring out the best in me."

Although it might have seemed abrupt, it wasn't. I had been thinking about bringing this up with Miki all week. The proper way to propose would have been to prepare her ring beforehand.

So I continued, "Let's go to New York next weekend to find rings for us!"

After what felt like long, drawn-out minutes, to my great relief, Miki looked at me with a bright smile and said, "Yes!"

True, it wasn't the most romantic proposal. There was no big event that people often prepare for a proposal. When I later told our daughter Sarah about the proposal, she seemed annoyed, saying, "How could you propose without kneeling or presenting a ring?"

Within two weeks of our decision to get married, we drove down to New York City to buy rings. We announced this to our parents, after which we all met to plan the engagement. Our engagement ceremony took place in October 1982 at our church in Rochester, with blessings from our family and friends. Two months later, in early December, we married at Flushing Methodist Church, where my parents were members. Despite it being early winter, the weather was mild, and we were able to go to the botanical garden nearby for our wedding photo shoot. Miki was twenty-three, and I was twenty-eight. We decided to get married without delay because I would be leaving for Chicago for a postdoc fellowship at the University of Chicago in January 1983, and we didn't want to be apart.

CHRISTMAS KIMCHI KIMBAP

I completed my PhD thesis defense in Rochester on December 20, 1982. I felt relieved, but it was also bittersweet. It felt like only a few weeks had passed since I came to Rochester to study, but five years had already passed and I had finally finished all the requirements for my PhD in biophysics. I had not paid a single cent to the school. It felt like a dream to have this opportunity. The only thing left was to attend commencement in May and receive my diploma.

My thesis defense happened to be the same night our church members were going Christmas caroling. Miki and I joined them. We all hopped into a van along with the pastor and other church members, visiting different families and singing carols at their doors. It was snowing lightly, creating a White Christmas atmosphere. It was four days before Christmas Eve. We drove from Pittsford to Fairport and other parts of Rochester, visiting church members' homes and singing "We Wish You a Merry Christmas." I remember some church members inviting us in to give us treats like pastries and drinks. In one of the elders' homes, the family treated us to roasted chestnuts, which reminded me of those I used to buy in the streets of Seoul many years before.

When we returned home after caroling, it was a little after midnight. *Alright, now my defense is finished!* I was still excited and couldn't fall asleep. This was understandable because I had waited so long for this moment and worked hard to achieve it. So many times while I was studying, I wondered if my efforts would pay off in the end. I ran into numerous obstacles during the experiments that made me question my work and left me wondering, *When will I ever finish this?* All these thoughts flooded my mind, and I was relieved that it was all finished.

Looking forward to our life in Chicago as a newly married couple, I felt giddy about the life ahead.

Miki seemed to read my mind. She smiled and said, "Hey, since we're not falling asleep, should we take a long drive to Chicago? You start work on January 5, but we haven't even found an apartment yet."

What she was saying made some sense. Chicago was six hundred miles away, but we seemed to have thought it was the next town over. I said, "Yeah, let's go!"

It was precisely 12:30 a.m., and we were hungry. We had to prepare something to eat on the way, and we decided kimbap would be perfect. Clever idea? But we had no ingredients except kimchi, so we made kimchi kimbap. We cooked rice and placed a sheet of seaweed on a board, and then we spread the rice evenly on the seaweed and topped it with chopped kimchi. We then rolled up the sheet and cut it into small rolls. What a simple process to create such a delicious treat! While I drove, Miki picked up a kimbap and put it in my mouth.

I said, "We must tell our future baby about this!"

Miki asked, "You mean about kimchi kimbap?"

"Yes," I replied. "About the fact we prepared kimbap at midnight on our way to Chicago. It's a brilliant idea!"

We laughed and continued eating kimbap and driving west toward our next adventure in Chicago.

MOVE TO CHICAGO

After a few days in Chicago, we came back to pack up for our move. We left Rochester on January 3, 1983. We had a small U-Haul trailer attached to the back of our car. Our friends came out to send us off and wish us luck. I still recall seeing them waving goodbye in my rearview mirror. It was a moment that completed my five years in Rochester.

We entered Ohio around dinnertime and decided to sleep at a hotel near Cleveland. We finally arrived in Chicago on the afternoon of January 4. We found an apartment on Blackstone Avenue in Hyde Park, near the University of Chicago campus. It was an old, art deco-style building but newly renovated the year before, so the inside was practically brand new. We lived in that one-bedroom apartment for the first six months before moving to a two-bedroom apartment in the same building, and such was the beginning of our newly wedded life.

It was an exciting time as we were planning all sorts of things for our future together. We had been married for exactly one month.

Marriage can bring many changes and adjustments for a couple. We were no longer dating; we were living in the same place as wife and husband. One thing that was a little strange, but I immediately got used to, was seeing Miki lying down next to me when I woke up in the morning. But marriage is much more than getting up together in the same bed. In retrospect, as newlyweds, we got along well with each other. We learned to adjust to each other's needs and relied on one another for happiness and stability.

We unpacked the boxes briskly and searched for our wedding gifts from our friends and relatives. Linens, beautiful china, and many pretty things for decorating the apartment. There was a Scandinavian furniture store within walking distance of our apartment where we purchased a bed, sofa, desks, and other accessories. We bought utensils and all the necessary kitchen stuff, and it was fun to decorate the apartment together.

Chicago was a completely new experience for Miki and me. We didn't have any friends or relatives there. The weather did not help either, as it was colder than Rochester in January. The strong wind blowing over Lake Michigan made the temperature even more frigid. But the two of us stayed warm because we had each other.

One day, we were walking on Clark Street on the north side of Chicago, looking at various stores, restaurants, and cafes. But because it was so cold, we wanted to escape into someplace warm. We found a quaint café close by. The café had limited seating options, with some tables and additional seats at the counter. We went in and took seats at the counter.

Miki said, "It smells good. I feel like having French onion soup."

We already had dinner at home, but we wanted something warm. "Sure, let's order two," I said.

But soon we realized we had enough money for only one, so

quickly we asked the waiter to give us one instead. I had no Visa or American Express Card then. The only credit card I had was a Sears card. Even that would often bounce due to late payments. We looked at each other and laughed about not having enough money to afford two soups. We shared the soup, which was still the best French onion soup ever. It's not like we were poor; we just didn't have enough money in the bank at that moment. But that was okay. We felt we were just perfect as long as we were together and we were able to work for our future. We had dreams; that was all we needed to forget any adversity.

RESEARCH AT THE UNIVERSITY OF CHICAGO

The campus at the University of Chicago was unique. In its center, buildings featured Gothic architecture. More contemporary buildings around the perimeter surrounded those buildings. I liked the classical atmosphere in the center best. When it snowed, Miki and I often went to a nearby cafe and admired the beautiful winter scenery around us.

I started my work there on January 6, 1983. My laboratory was in a building separate from the hospital, where all the basic science labs were. I met my advisor Dr. Michael Field and his staff members. There were five people with PhDs or MDs, and two of them were gastroenterologists.

The University of Chicago is well known for its pure academics and research, similar to the schools I attended previously. Many preeminent researchers came from various parts of the US and the world to study there. The research environment was excellent, and I had the opportunity to meet researchers from diverse backgrounds. This experience expanded my knowledge and expertise in science.

In my laboratory, I used large intestinal cells isolated from rabbits as a model to investigate the effects of neurohumoral agents on transcellular electrolyte transport. My research went smoothly, and in January 1984, just about a year after I moved to Chicago, I published my third paper in the *American Journal of Physiology*.

Although I was generally happy with my work, I always had medical school in the back of my mind. I had already finished graduate school and was now doing my postdoc fellowship. It dawned on me that I should go to medical school before it was too late. Then I learned there was a PhD-to-MD program at the University of Miami Miller School of Medicine. This program offered an MD in two years to qualified students with PhDs in biomedical sciences.

Two years, not four! I thought. The first group of classes in the PhD-to-MD program would start in May and end in December, followed by the initial US Medical Licensing Examination. This first exam was equivalent to the test administered after the first two years of traditional medical school. The PhD-to-MD program applicants were mainly PhDs in biology and physical sciences, so the coursework covered during the first two years of a traditional four-year program was already familiar to them. The following eighteen months of the program would involve clinical rotations with third- and fourth-year medical students from the regular four-year program.

TRIBUTE TO MY MENTOR

PhD-to-MD was an extremely competitive program because only thirty applicants were selected out of several hundred. I had some doubts about getting in, but I submitted my application on February 14, 1984, one day before the deadline. I thought about asking my advisor, Dr. Field, to write a recommendation letter on my behalf. Coincidentally, Dr. Field called me into his office around this time and told me Columbia University offered him a position as chief of gastroenterology. He asked me to come along with him. I didn't know what to say. It was a dilemma because I had just submitted my application, and I was about to ask Dr. Field to write me a recommendation letter.

I finally summoned the courage to bring this up to Dr. Field, but I couldn't help being nervous. I knocked at his office door and heard him saying, "Come in," in the distance. He was in the middle of writing, looked up, and asked, "What's up, Chul?" He must have sensed something unusual from the expression on my face. He put his pen on the desk and looked at me curiously. "Come on in and have a seat."

I sat and said, "Mike, I have something to ask you for. As you know, I've wanted to go to medical school for many years, and I just applied. I need a recommendation letter. Can you help me?"

He did not seem surprised since he was already familiar with my background. He knew I intended to go to medical school. Looking at me intently, he paused for what felt like a long time. Then, finally, he smiled and said, "Hmm … I see. Which schools are you applying to?"

"University of Miami," I said. "That's the only school I am applying to." I briefly explained the PhD-to-MD program.

After another pause, Dr. Field said, "I understand. I'll do whatever I can to help you. I have a good friend who did a residency with me years ago, and he has been a faculty member at Miami for a while. He is a great guy. I'll write to him."

I felt so relieved; however, I still find it surprising that he asked only a few questions. He knew me and understood what I wanted to do in the future. He probably read my mind. It was tough for me to ask him since I had worked in his laboratory for only a little more than a year. But he was very patient, always listening to all my stories and willing to help me. I was so thankful, and I still cannot forget the smile he gave me.

Someone once told me that our lives are determined by who we meet. I have met many people in my life, and without their help or influence, I don't think I could have done half of what I have accomplished so far. This includes Miki and some of my teachers. Dr. Michael Field at the University of Chicago was one of these people. I first met him in the summer of 1982 when I was wrapping up my PhD thesis. I was visiting several universities around the country to look for a postdoctoral fellowship position. My first impression of him was that he was warm and gentle. Although it was the first time we met, I could tell he was somebody I could easily open up to and have honest conversations with. My interview with him was formal, but I remember most of our conversations were about my life and background.

Dr. Field never seemed to get upset, even when we encountered difficulties in the lab. Instead, he would smile and say, "Okay, let's do this again." The composure and grace with which he approached life remain an inspiration to me. I ran into Dr. Field several times after I left

Chicago, once during my residency at Georgetown and another time when I visited his laboratory at Columbia to finish some experiments. And I occasionally saw him at conferences. Several years ago, I heard the sad news that Dr. Field passed away at his residence in Maine. As a man of high integrity and warmth, he was a true mentor to me and many others. He will be greatly missed.

SUCCESS AND SACRIFICE

While I was leading a busy life in and out of laboratories in Chicago, Miki enrolled at the University of Illinois Department of Architecture. She studied fine art in college and worked at an architect's office in Rochester after graduation, which motivated her to study architecture. Given the intimate relationship between art and architecture, her decision to pursue architecture was a natural transition. The two of us led hectic lives in pursuit of our passions.

During our weekends when we had some free time, we went for walks, drove along Lake Shore Drive, explored downtown, and cherished our moments together. We often visited bookstores and coffee shops. In December 1983, for our first wedding anniversary, I surprised Miki with dinner at a prestigious French restaurant near Water Tower Place in downtown Chicago. I remember paying about $150 for our meal, which turned out to be more than 10 percent of my salary. We settled in nicely though, adjusting well to our new surroundings. We were fortunate to make friends with amazing people from both the University of Chicago and Northwestern University. Miki and I were choir members at our church on Lawrence Avenue on Chicago's North Side, where we met people who became lifelong friends.

Finally, two months after I submitted my application to the University of Miami, the school wanted to interview me. Miki and

I were so excited we could hardly sleep. When the call came, I was busy preparing for the American Gastroenterological Association conference in early May in New Orleans. The University of Miami informed me that one of its alumni, a faculty member at the Tulane School of Medicine, would interview me in New Orleans. So I went to New Orleans, had a good interview, and returned to Chicago. My second interview was with another alumnus, a psychiatrist practicing in Chicago. Finally, one week after my second interview, I received a phone call from the dean saying, "Chul, congratulations on your acceptance!" I couldn't believe what I heard. It didn't feel real.

I called Miki immediately and shared the news. We were so exhilarated we couldn't sleep that night. The next day, full of thoughts, not knowing what to anticipate, Miki and I started to pack. It was around May 15, and classes were starting on May 28. That gave us two weeks to move to Miami and find an apartment. But then, while I went to school for the next two years, what would Miki do? Would she be able to continue her studies there? We had already discussed this many times. Now, it had become a reality, and we had to make up our minds. Miki had just finished her first year of graduate school at the University of Illinois. It would be ideal for her to continue her education in Miami. But there was no school of architecture in Miami. So she would take a leave of absence for the next two years and instead work in an architectural firm in Miami. It was one of many sacrifices Miki made to accommodate my career.

BACK TO MY MED SCHOOL DREAM

Miki and I sent all our belongings to the moving center around May 20. We planned a three-day, two-night drive to Miami. Since I would be swamped starting in June, we thought we could use the remaining time to travel and enjoy each other's company. After leaving Chicago, we arrived at the Smoky Mountains in Gatlinburg, Tennessee, in about eight hours. We spent the night there and left for Florida the following day. We passed through the hills of Georgia and entered the flat land of Florida, where we spent the night in a hotel. Then, early the next morning, we left for Miami before the sun was up.

When we started traveling in Florida, we immediately noticed the lush vegetation and vibrant, colorful flowers we could never imagine seeing in Chicago. Miki repeatedly exclaimed, "Wow, so beautiful!" I was thinking about how busy I would be with my studies for the next two years, but I was soon comforted that at least Miki would be able to enjoy the beautiful surroundings. After all, I know her love and passion for plants and flowers. We also felt liberated from the atrociously cold, blizzardy, winter weather of Chicago and welcomed the warmth of Florida's sunny days.

Nevertheless, we were grateful for the life we built in Chicago. When we arrived in Chicago, we knew no one. But in a year and a half, I met one of my most incredible mentors. I conducted valuable research with good outcomes. And we made lifelong friends in Chicago. Miki clarified her professional goal of becoming an architect. And now I was going for my goal of becoming a physician. This was a dream come true.

All sorts of flowers bloom throughout the year in Miami, including unusual tropical plants and flowers that Miki and I had never seen before. To Miki, Florida was heaven.

The vast, blue sea near Miami and its clean air and roads are world famous. In addition to the ocean, two other aspects add to the culture: Cuba and Hemingway. In the '70s, many Cubans fled their country, settling in Miami to free themselves from Fidel Castro. Cuban culture is prominent in Miami through food, art, music, language, and more. Key West, which is only two hours away from Miami, is famous for being the home of Hemingway during the last years of his life.

When we arrived in Miami, we slept one night in a hotel near the school. The next day we started looking for an apartment. Unfortunately, we didn't have time to look before then, but we weren't worried, figuring we would be able to find one in a few days. We were lucky to discover a condominium located in Kendall, an area that is a forty-five-minute commute from school. Our belongings arrived the next day, and we spent time unpacking, organizing, and moving in. It was time to go to school soon. After finishing registration, I started classes on May 28, 1984.

FAST-TRACK MD PROGRAM

There were precisely thirty students in the class. The average age was thirty-two, two years older than my age then. On average, these students had finished four years of postdoctoral training. Seven of them were already faculty members in their universities. They were mature and serious about their studies. Since we planned to finish the first two years of medical school in seven months, the pace of the courses had to be fast. Our classes went from 8:00 a.m. to 6:00 p.m. on weekdays, with additional classes held on Saturdays until 2:00 p.m. Whenever I felt tired, I used to go to a snack bar and order a Cuban espresso with extra sugar.

I carpooled with two other classmates. Since it took forty-five minutes to commute, we used this time to study and quiz each other. I didn't have a lot of time to exercise, but I would dive into our pool and swim when I came home from school.

Because of my busy schedule, there were many weekends I could not go to church with Miki, but on Saturday and Sunday evenings we would go out to eat, take walks, and enjoy our time together.

Miki found an architectural firm where she could work as an intern. During her time at that company, she made several good friends and gained valuable hands-on experience.

CONNECTING WITH CUBAN IMMIGRANTS

During my time in Miami, I had the opportunity to meet and get to know Cuban Americans. Some of my classmates were children of parents who immigrated from Cuba. The flux of Cuban immigrants took place even before the Cuban Revolution, which ended in 1959. Since then, there have been several waves of immigrants from Cuba. Most of them found new homes in Southern Florida centered around Miami. In the early '80s, I saw many Cuban immigrants establishing their communities. This was when I had close contact with Cuban culture and history. It is interesting to note that the timing of Cuban immigration closely parallels that of Korean immigrants.

I witnessed the struggles of my Cuban friends and their families to settle in a new country. Those setbacks and hardships are not different from the ones I have seen with my parents and others in the Asian American community. Like immigrants from Korea, Cuban immigrants had difficulty learning a new language and overcoming ethnic discrimination. In the face of social and other fundamental inequities, they had to work hard to forge a unique cultural identity. I related Cuban American issues to my own experiences and family. And I came to understand them. We can grow closer and more familiar when we share these commonalities among our backgrounds and interests with others.

REAL-WORLD INSIGHTS

Time flew by fast. Seven months passed, and it was time for the first Medical Licensing Exam. Every one of my thirty classmates passed, so we all had a good Christmas and New Year. My clinical rotations started in January, and my first rotation was in psychiatry. Looking back, having psychiatry as my first rotation was fortuitous because it required all aspects of clinical tools, including diagnostic imaging and blood tests. One of the essential tools in psychiatry is interviewing patients, a crucial element that allows human interaction with patients. Sadly, we are increasingly lacking human touch in the medical specialties that rely heavily on blood tests, imaging, and artificial intelligence-based technology. Compared to other fields, psychiatry places a greater emphasis on the narratives provided by patients.

In this rotation, I learned to conduct patient interviews. My professor would engage in conversations with patients to learn about them. I observed how he led the discussions, the kinds of questions he asked, and his observations. In some cases, starting or continuing discussions with patients was challenging. But I gradually learned to listen and tried to understand the conversation holistically.

I would first introduce myself. Then, I would ask, "How are you feeling?" or "What brings you here?" or "Is there anything bothering you?" These open-ended questions are good icebreakers to invite patients to say a few things about themselves in any way they like. I tried to make them as comfortable as possible so they could be less uptight. But no matter how much we try, communication with non-English-speaking patients is often hindered by linguistic and cultural differences.

One patient said, "I'm afraid to speak with non-Spanish-speaking doctors. I don't know how to describe the symptoms I have. I fear there will be misunderstandings both ways." And there are issues with intercultural misunderstanding. One Chinese patient said, "My doctor told me I must come to the clinic at least two times a year for a checkup. But I am doing fine, so I chose not to return to the clinic. I do not see why I need a checkup unless I have a symptom."

I had to consider the patients' different linguistic and sociocultural backgrounds. There is so much more to clinical medicine than just science. With rapid advances in science and technology during the past several decades, physicians rely on them more heavily than ever before. As a result, doctors spend significantly less time interacting with patients at the bedside.

We are halfway there if doctors listen to patients and understand their complaints. It is crucial to see things from patients' perspectives. But how often do doctors do that? I often question if we, as physicians, are good listeners. Even after nearly thirty years of practice, I still need to improve as a listener. I find myself cutting patients short while they are talking. Either I believe that I already know what my patients will say or that it may not matter what they have to say because I have already decided what to do for them.

All aspects of clinical investigations and diagnostic testing start from the first meeting between the patient and the doctor. Therefore, this session requires clear and effective communication.

Rotations in internal medicine, OB/GYN, surgery, and others followed. Among these, I found internal medicine most appealing. I liked the logical processes applied in evaluating patients' problems and the step-by-step approach to finding solutions. I especially liked endocrinology, rheumatology, and gastroenterology. However, I was most attracted to gastroenterology (GI), and this was because I had spent the past seven years researching small and large intestinal epithelial cells. I decided to specialize in internal medicine and go into the GI subspecialty.

Among many heartbreaking interactions I will never forget from my clinical clerkships were my encounters with AIDS patients. AIDS became an epidemic in Miami, making it one of the first cities in the US to be affected. The city already had a high prevalence of venereal diseases, and AIDS followed suit. Many patients died during the height of the epidemic, and as physicians, we were helpless. Today there are effective treatments for AIDS, and AIDS is no longer classified as a terminal disease but as a chronic disease. But in the '80s, it was a disease with a death sentence.

INTERNSHIP DESTINATION

The winter of 1985 was busy. I visited a number of university hospitals for internship interviews. Finally, in April 1986, the National Resident Matching Program announced which hospital I would be matched with, determining my fate for the next three years. That day, Miki came to school to join me to find out my match. We anxiously awaited these results.

Georgetown! Oh wow! It was one of my top choices, and I was pleased and relieved. It felt like the past two years just flew by. When tired or frustrated, I had lamented, "When am I ever going to be done?" And now, graduation day was quickly approaching.

I graduated from medical school in May 1986. It was the moment I had been waiting for so long. But then I quickly realized that was not the end. I had to do a residency, followed by a fellowship, which would take six years altogether. And who knew what was waiting for me after that? *Where is the finish line? Or is there one?* I thought. All I knew was that I was on a long path with a finish line far away. The trick to surviving on this journey was making the best out of whatever I faced. I had to get used to accepting new challenges with humility and gratitude.

JUST KEEP THE PACE—YOUR PACE

I enrolled at the University of Miami Miller School of Medicine in May 1984, seven years later than my classmates from college. However, since I was able to finish medical school in two years, I became a physician five years later than my undergraduate classmates who went to medical school straight out of college. Of course, I also had done my PhD and a postdoctoral fellowship in those seven years. When I finished my fellowship, it was 1992, and I was thirty-eight. Initially, I was disappointed that I would become a specialist at that age. But as I got older, I realized five years is a small portion of your lifetime. And remember, time flies by, especially when you are doing something meaningful. If you wasted time in the past, do not worry. With a clear goal and perseverance, you can still make up for lost time. Regrettably, some people may feel hesitant to pursue new career paths or education opportunities due to their age or past setbacks. Whatever they experienced in the past, good or bad, can be significant assets for the future. It is entirely up to you how to make use of that past. Who is to say what is good and bad?

Life is a marathon, not a short-distance race. The goal is to enjoy the running and finish safe. Just because you start running slowly doesn't mean you will finish last. And even if you finish last, it's much better than not finishing. It's important to remind yourself that you don't have to run faster than others. We are competitive by nature, but a marathon is a race with yourself more than a race against others.

I recall an episode during a marathon in New Jersey about seventeen years ago. My target finish time was four hours and twenty minutes, meaning I had to run ten-minute miles. I planned to finish the first thirteen miles in two hours and the second thirteen miles in two hours and twenty minutes. Around the nine-mile point, I saw a lady running with a big sign on her back that said "Grandma." To me, that sign was an invitation to pass her by! Although her posture seemed a bit lopsided, she appeared to be in good shape for her age.

After running behind her consistently for a while, I felt confident and thought to myself, *I am fifty-two, and she is a grandma. I'd better run faster than her!* So, I passed her. But that moment of victory was brief because she passed me before I knew it! For the next few miles, Grandma and I did this dance of continually passing each other. Finally, I let her go past me. The cramps in my quads became so bad that I had to mostly walk for the remainder of the race, finishing a whole hour later than I had expected. This was a lesson in humility for me.

That was more than one hundred marathons ago. Running has allowed me to discover and push my physical and psychological limits while teaching me humility. We learn to run at our own pace, not those imposed by others. And in this particular run, I discovered another worthy lesson: "Do not judge a book by its cover."

The speed at which you complete your goals does not define your success in life. What matters is how well you finish and if you are content with that. The goal is to keep your own pace and be true to it, and whether others around you run faster should not matter. And similarly, running faster than others is not a reason to be arrogant. Again, don't get stressed because you are running slower than other people. Go at your own pace, and be happy with it.

Whether or not we succeed in our lives is not determined by something that takes place in one or two moments. I have learned from marathons that life is a long journey. Enjoy it the best you can. If you face obstacles, you can go around them. Keep your own pace. It's okay to be late. Actually, you won't be.

ADVANCING CAREERS IN METRO DC

Miki and I wrapped up our two years in Miami and moved to DC in June 1986. We sent all our belongings and took a road trip up the East

Coast toward DC. We had become experts in packing and moving. We had two cars, and my sister-in-law Mihea came from New York to help us. Mihea and Miki drove one car, and I drove the other. Our first stop was Orlando, where we stayed at our friend's house and had dinner. Then we headed toward Charleston, South Carolina, our second stop the next day. After that, we went sightseeing and headed toward Arlington, Virginia, where our new home awaited. It was our first home in DC.

We lived in three different places during my residency in Georgetown. In my first year, when I was swamped as an intern, we lived in Arlington, only a few miles away from the medical center. In my second year, we lived in Beltsville, Maryland; in the third, we lived in McLean, Virginia. Summers in DC were sweltering and oppressive. In many ways, it was worse than the heat of Miami. In Miami, no matter where you went, there was always air conditioning, and all the apartments had pools where you could cool off. But in DC, the heat was relentless. There were no pools or beaches. The temperature would rise to one hundred degrees. One day Miki and I picked up a giant watermelon from the grocery store and finished it in one sitting. We spent that night taking turns in the bathroom, and neither of us slept. Even today, when we think of Arlington, we think of the watermelon and laugh.

BUSTLING GEORGETOWN UNIVERSITY MEDICAL CENTER

Georgetown University Medical Center was significantly smaller than Jackson Memorial Hospital, where I had been trained as a medical student. Despite its small size, it was a bustling hospital where I could never get a good night's sleep whenever I was on call because of numerous admissions throughout the night. This was a great learning environment, exposing me to a broad spectrum of clinical cases.

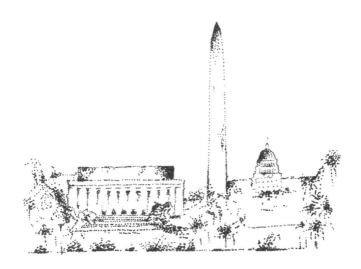

Georgetown differed significantly from Miami in many other ways. Miami was liberal concerning the dress code and the social scene, but Georgetown was more conservative. Etiquette mattered. For example, Georgetown enforced dress policies. We all wore neckties and had to pay more attention to our demeanor while with patients. It was understandable, as a traditional dress code and manners project a more professional image and help to strengthen reputation.

My first rotation as an intern was oncology. There I witnessed so many of the limitations of medicine. We had twenty-four beds in the oncology unit, and most patients came in to get chemotherapy. Since a majority of these patients had advanced cancer, the prognosis was poor. I learned how to approach and talk to patients and their family members in difficult situations. I observed that among many terminal cancer patients nearing death, some accepted their imminent death in a surprisingly calm manner. On the other hand, many others were depressed and in agony. With incurable diseases and death approaching for these patients, what can physicians offer? It was especially sad when I faced young adolescent patients dying from leukemia.

Residency is a critical transition period from student to full-fledged physician. My experiences at Georgetown helped me transition smoothly. The quality and safety of patient care depend on this preparation. Many memorable moments arose during my clinic duties on general medicine floors, the Cardiac Care Unit, and Intensive Care Unit. I made numerous mistakes, and I gradually learned it was okay to admit the mistakes—the earlier, the better, and the safer for patients. It was challenging, and acknowledging that I made a mistake did not come easily. However, the important thing is to correct errors quickly.

MIKI'S RETURN TO GRAD SCHOOL

During my second year as a resident, Miki resumed her studies, enrolling as a graduate student in the Department of Architecture at the University of Maryland in College Park. Although our home in Beltsville was far from Georgetown, it was perfect for Miki's commute. Her school life was hectic. It was an exciting but challenging milestone. She went to school in the morning and came home late at night, staying up many nights in her studio to finish projects. Dedicated to her success, she studied a lot more and harder than I did in medical school. At the end of each semester, Miki was required to present her final projects to a panel of critics consisting of her professors and classmates. The days leading up to her presentations were nothing short of intense.

My schedule wasn't any lighter. I was on call every third night. And in between those nights, I was moonlighting. There were many weeks when I didn't come home for two days in a row. When I came home, I would sleep one night and be on call the next day. I always carried spare socks, undershirts, and shirts in my bag. Miki and I could have dinner together only once or twice a week. Although we were tired, we felt grateful for the opportunities to pursue our dreams.

I had more free time as I was starting my third year of residency. So I took a look around Washington, DC. While we had already been living in DC for two years, I had seen only a little in the area besides the hospitals and my home. Unlike Miki, who was already knowledgeable about the museums in DC, I had yet to visit the Smithsonian National Museum of Natural History, National Gallery of Art, and other notable museums. Who would believe me if I told them I had never seen these places after living there for nearly three years?

MAKING CHOICES FOR FAMILY AND CAREER

One day, I received a call from my parents in the middle of my internship. My father developed anemia due to GI bleeding, and his doctor recommended an endoscopy right away. I asked my dad to come to the Georgetown University Hospital the next day. After the endoscopy and CT scans, he was diagnosed with stomach cancer. I discussed the finding with my brother, who at the time was in Korea. My father flew to Seoul the following week and underwent surgery at Seoul National

University Hospital. Because stomach cancers are far more prevalent in Korea than in the US, doctors there have more clinical experience treating stomach cancer than anywhere else. My brother and I wanted our dad to be taken care of by the most experienced doctors. Fortunately, it was early-stage cancer, and he recovered uneventfully after the surgery.

My third year in residency was full of electives. It was time for a fellowship application. I searched for an appropriate fellowship program that would be aligned with my decision to pursue a career as a gastroenterologist. The fellowship application was similar to the residency application in that I listed the programs by preference and waited for a school to select me.

My top choices were Yale New Haven Hospital and Harvard's Massachusetts General Hospital. I indicated Yale as my first choice. There were two reasons I liked Yale more. First, Yale had a great tradition in the field of epithelial transport, which I did research in. Dr. Henry Binder at Yale was a world-renowned scientist in large intestinal transport, and he later became my mentor. Because my previous research focused on the intestine, I believed it would be beneficial for my academic career to continue research in that area. Second, Harvard's GI programs were separated into several hospitals: Massachusetts General Hospital, Brigham and Women's Hospital, and Beth Israel Deaconess Medical Center. In contrast, Yale had one solid program, combining Yale New Haven Hospital with West Haven VA Medical Center. Yale also had a larger faculty and a greater diversity of expertise. Yale chose me in the match, and Miki and I started our plans to move to New Haven in June. As I finished my residency at Georgetown, Miki also completed her graduate work in Maryland, earning an MA in Architecture.

"Oh wow, it's time to pack again!" I said.

"I wonder how New Haven is going to be?" Miki responded.

I replied, "There is only one way to find out."

We looked at each other and laughed.

IT'S GO TIME ... AGAIN

We finalized our three years in DC and headed to the town of Hamden, Connecticut, just north of New Haven, in June 1989. We sold our condominium in McLean and used this money to purchase a small house.

The first home Miki and I bought was at 65 Ingram Street in Hamden, immediately north of New Haven. Our house was on a cul-de-sac, and it faced a small lake. The backyard was not well arranged and did not live up to Miki's perfectionist ways, but we knew it would improve with some work. The problem was the house itself. While the house looked fine outside, the interior needed a lot of work. The main bedroom needed to be gutted and renovated, and a bathroom and the kitchen required updates. It looked like an almost impossible living space unless we did a lot of repairs. But Miki and I were still happy. We liked the fireplace, the early twentieth-century design, and the lake view we could see from our dining room through a huge window. We felt hopeful that the house could be converted into something beautiful if we did some work and redesigning. And we were excited about all the possibilities for our new home.

Miki was hired by a world-famous architecture firm in New Haven, Roche and Dinkeloo. I don't think there were many women architects then. When Miki joined the firm in 1989, there was only one other woman architect at Roche and Dinkeloo.

Roche and Dinkeloo employed about one hundred people, and

the chief architect was Kevin Roche, a renowned architect originally from Ireland. He was a Pritzker Architecture Prize recipient, and he and his firm designed the Ford Foundation, the Oakland Museum of California, New York's Metropolitan Museum of Art, and other landmark buildings. Mr. Roche was calm and gentle. I met him a few times, and until he passed away at ninety-six, he maintained his humble character and continued to work. Miki was fortunate to work with such a great mentor and build up her experience under his guidance.

At our home, Miki and I did some construction little by little. Our first project was to renovate the two bathrooms and the kitchen. We hired a carpenter, but Miki and I did simple things like the demolition. I purchased a small truck, and whenever I was free in the evenings, I would drive to Home Depot to buy sheetrock and other materials for the carpenter to work with the next day. We did this to save money, but we also took joy in creating a space that was our home. Miki would invite her architect colleagues to our house and get advice on design and construction. We were delighted because it was our first home.

I was busy at the hospital on weekdays but had some free time on weekends. My life became more leisurely than when I was a resident. With my fellowship and Miki's salary, we could live without significant financial difficulties. But it was not enough to start paying back the loans accumulated in the past fifteen years. So I worked at night once a week, which helped us financially. On weekends, we attended New Haven Methodist Church, where Miki's brother, Jong, was a pastor.

ENRICHING ENCOUNTERS AT YALE

Located near Hartford and Stamford, New Haven has led Connecticut's commerce, culture, and education. Yale University was founded in 1701, and its campus occupies about half of the city of

New Haven, so it is tough to say if Yale is in New Haven or if New Haven is in Yale.

In my first year as a fellow, I rotated through Yale New Haven Hospital, Saint Raphael Hospital, and West Haven VA Medical Center. Yale is an excellent institution that excels in basic science research, and the school is full of world-famous scholars and academic traditions. Yale provided a perfect environment to bring together basic and clinical investigators to work for common goals. This was an enriching year when I encountered many fascinating gastrointestinal and liver disease cases. Starting with typical GI bleeding cases from peptic ulcer diseases and other sources, I saw many patients with chronic liver diseases with complications of portal hypertension. Management of variceal bleeds and ascites was often challenging. As one of the first liver study centers in the US, Yale allowed me to witness some of the most uncommon liver cases. The liver diseases library, equipped with numerous microscopic specimens from the rarest liver diseases worldwide, was most impressive.

I learned endoscopy, a procedure involving inserting a long, flexible tube with a camera, called an endoscope, to examine the esophagus, stomach, and small and large intestines. As a graduate student and postdoctoral fellow, I worked on various intestinal cell models, investigating how ion and glucose molecules can move across these cells from lumen to blood. The fact that I could enter a human body to see the moving organ by advancing an endoscope brought sheer excitement. Looking at an actively moving organ and evaluating any possible abnormality was an awakening experience. While witnessing the connections between the cells and tissue, tissue to organ, and organ to an entire body, I began to appreciate and imagine how my research at the bench may translate into patients lying in hospital beds.

I had fewer clinical duties in my second and third years. Instead, I was occupied with research and doing experiments. Based on my research goals, I decided to join Dr. Binder's laboratory to study the regulation of electrolyte transport. While I utilized intestinal models from chickens and rabbits in the past, at Yale I used mice's large intestines as a model to examine electrolyte transport. My research topics were related to understanding the regulation of cellular electrolyte transport processes in inflammatory diarrheal diseases, as seen in Crohn's disease and ulcerative colitis. I studied the mechanisms of leukotriene, prostaglandin, and other inflammatory markers on the electrolyte transport across large intestinal cells. Afterward, these studies were published in the *American Journal of Physiology*. This was a crucial period in my life because the work I accomplished during these two years shaped my future path in academic medicine. Moreover, having the opportunity to work with a great mentor was an enriching experience.

Time flew by. As I was approaching my third year as a fellow, it was time to look for a job. I had always dreamed of becoming an academic physician, so I looked around the country for these positions. I visited New York, Texas, Iowa, Wisconsin, and the medical schools in these states for interviews. Finally, after many discussions with Miki, we decided moving to New York, where our families were, would be best. I took a job as an assistant professor at Stony Brook School of Medicine on Long Island. In addition, I would be working as an attending physician at Winthrop University Hospital in Mineola, New York (now renamed NYU Langone Hospital—Long Island).

So in June 1992, it was time to wrap up our lives in New Haven and move to New York. I always felt sorry for Miki because of our moving around; she was forced to quit her schooling and her jobs. Also, we were sad to leave the house we had become attached to and leave our church and friends. It was sad to have to repeat goodbyes. But the place we would move to now was where Miki grew up and our parents both lived, so these factors comforted us in overcoming the sadness of leaving our home in Connecticut.

Ah, now all my studies are done, I thought. From my freshman year in 1973 when I arrived in the United States until the summer of 1992, exactly nineteen years had passed. I thought, *I am now entering the real world.* I believed this was the end of my long race through educational institutions. Little did I know there were other races ahead in my future.

BACK TO NEW YORK

As an attending physician at Winthrop University Hospital, I had fellows, residents, and students under my charge. A few weeks before, I was just a fellow, and overnight, I became an attending physician with more significant responsibilities. It was kind of weird but also a proud moment to make rounds in the hospital with them. But these moments of awkwardness soon disappeared, and I became used to life as an attending physician.

Miki also found a great job at an architectural firm with five other architects in Oyster Bay, Long Island. The firm specialized in building medical facilities, including hospitals and imaging centers. Miki acquired valuable insights about designing health-care spaces. She met new peers, some of whom she still collaborates with today.

My duties in the hospital involved seeing both inpatients and outpatients and performing procedures. In addition, I had academic responsibilities, including teaching fellows and conducting research. I devoted two days a week to basic science research.

SAYING GOODBYE TO MY DAD

When Miki and I settled in Long Island for my position with Winthrop University Hospital, my parents were living in New Haven. Unfortunately, my father was diagnosed with laryngeal cancer in 1994 and underwent chemotherapy at Yale New Haven Hospital. This was his second cancer after his stomach cancer, which had been successfully treated with surgery ten years prior. We thought he had a remarkable response to chemotherapy, and his doctor was confident of his prognosis. But six months after therapy, my father felt a large lump protruding on the right side of his belly. It turned out to be a metastatic lesion on his liver. He was now diagnosed with metastatic cancer.

"Now I don't have much time to live," my dad said, disappointed and depressed. But despite this dismal reality, my father managed to keep his composure. "This is God's will. I am okay, and don't you guys worry," he said. He wanted to visit his younger sister in San Francisco, so I quickly arranged for my parents to travel there to see her.

He returned after a week's trip and became gravely ill. As he lay dying, I felt helpless. There was nothing I could do for my dad. Miki started to sing a hymn, and my mother and I followed.

> When peace, like a river, attendeth my way,
> When sorrows like sea billows roll;
> Whatever my lot, Thou hast taught me to say,
> It is well, it is well with my soul.

It was Dad's favorite hymn. I wondered if he could hear us sing. We sang to comfort my dad and ease our own sadness and loss. I glanced over at my mother and saw that she was crying softly, perhaps feeling the same regrets I was. She was losing her life companion of fifty years.

"Mom, you have been great to Dad, especially these past few years when he was ill," I said.

Miki, my mother, and I were with him when he passed. He was unconscious, and his breath was getting shorter and shallower each time he breathed with agony. Finally, he took his last breath and was gone.

Is this how my dad's life ends? I couldn't stop thinking about the emptiness of life. He had sacrificed his life in many ways, leaving his comfortable job in Korea for the sake of his children. *I am sorry, Dad. I should have been a better son*, I thought. I felt guilty for many things I had not done as his son. I regretted not visiting my dad more frequently while he was alive. Should I have stopped my studies, found a job, and tried to help my parents financially? I didn't do that. Maybe I was too selfish and focused on my own life. Seeing my dad lifeless on the bed, I felt empty and desperately sorry for not being a better son.

My father was not rich, yet he always wanted to do something for us. "Is there anything you need? I am sorry," he would always say. It was clear that he regretted not being able to provide us with certain things.

I would say, "No problem. I am at school and don't need any money." While he may not have been able to provide in worldly ways, he was always by my side cheering me on through my studies and life's goals.

I remember my father as a true gentleman. He was a loving father to his sons. He taught and showed us how to live humble and honest lives. When I visited New Haven to see him, I often found him sitting and quietly reading the Bible in the town's public library. I would approach him, and his face would brighten as soon as he saw me. He had the same smile when visiting me at Johns Hopkins years ago. I did not fully appreciate how happy my presence could make him. *Does my face light up the same way when I see my daughter Sarah visiting me?* I wondered.

VI.
TACKLING
A NEW
CAREER
CHALLENGE

BRINGING CARE TO MY COMMUNITY

During my time as an attending physician at Winthrop University Hospital in Mineola, New York, my office was conveniently located only a half hour away from Queens. Korean patients sought me out, coming from Flushing and other parts of New York City. A majority of these patients had language and cultural barriers in accessing care from English-speaking providers. Although there were numerous Korean patients suffering from liver and other digestive diseases, there were only a few Korean-speaking gastroenterologists in New York. So I opened an office in New York City to accommodate the growing Korean patient population. Some patients had stomach cancer, and others came with severe complications of viral hepatitis B, such as liver cancer and cirrhosis. I was surprised to learn that these diseases affecting the Korean population were often discovered at a late stage, when there were limited or no treatment options available. I learned later that the majority of Korean patients avoided preventative checkups because of their busy lives as immigrants. Even with symptoms, they often would not seek medical attention.

REACHING OUT THROUGH PRIVATE PRACTICE

After much thought and analysis, I opened medical practices in the Flushing neighborhood in Queens and in Midtown Manhattan. Both areas have large populations of Koreans. It was April 1996. I specialized in internal medicine and gastroenterology. This transition from academic medicine to private practice was unexpectedly complex. I felt lost at first. As an academic physician, I had divided my hours between clinical work and research. Academic medicine had been my lifelong dream. I had always felt my calling was in research, but now I was practicing full-time clinical medicine. I felt regretful that I couldn't do basic science research. But my dream and objectives in life slowly changed as I began to serve the Korean community. I felt inspired knowing I was able to help others. The practice grew, and I moved my Flushing office to Englewood Cliffs, New Jersey, a few years later.

This was the beginning of a new chapter in my life. I became affiliated with Weill Cornell Medical School as an assistant professor and obtained admitting privileges at New York Hospital (now known as Weill Cornell Medical Center). My responsibilities included teaching, seeing inpatients along with residents, and supervising fellows in endoscopies.

CHALLENGES AND REWARDS

Opening my medical practice was a challenging process. In retrospect, however, it is one of the most rewarding things I have ever done. While I understood my role on the academic and clinical side, I had no experience in administrative aspects such as reimbursement and cost management. It was the mid-1990s when HMOs and managed care were actively emerging in the US health-care market. Managed care, in turn, caused changes in the organization and dynamics of health systems, creating confusion among all the stakeholders. As a result, I had little idea of how to manage my practice correctly. Once I opened my business account and started to run the office, it was a new world for me.

Understanding the insurance payer system was a crucial task. After all, this is how providers get paid. The amount and consistency of payments determined my financial success and the durability of my medical practice. Regrettably, payment procedures have become increasingly complex, placing excessive demands on administrative tasks and diverting attention and time away from patient care. These increased requirements cause significant stress and burnout among physicians.

In addition to the business side, I had to get involved with all aspects of office management, including hiring receptionists, billing clerks, and nurses. I also had to build the right culture for my team and come up with ways to enhance professional satisfaction. I concentrated on nurses' education and providing the best care for my patients. Since I started offering office-based endoscopy, I managed all the endoscopy-related factors, such as nurse training and purchasing endoscopy-related supplies and materials.

As a private practitioner, my outlook toward patients and medicine changed. As an attending physician at the hospital, I was performing procedures in a hospital endoscopy center surrounded by fellows, residents, and nurses. All the ancillary supports were readily available. As a private practitioner, however, I was facing a sedated patient alone in an office with only one nurse beside me. What would I do if something happened to the patient? All the support and comforts of academia and the university medical center were now gone. It was nerve-racking, to say the least.

But I practiced taking things as they came, and luckily, I learned to adapt to a new environment and embrace challenges in the most positive ways I could. It was a great learning experience that I would never have gained without being placed in the situation.

What I enjoyed the most about private practice was my autonomy. I was at peace on my own, and I could be creative in my patients' care. There were no interruptions by institutions or third parties. I didn't have to go through five different committees to get permission to do a small thing. In my practice, I would sit down with my staff members, and if we decided to do something differently, we could make the change overnight. Having a private practice helped me think independently and develop a sense of ownership where I could control the trajectory of my life and my visions for the future. Having experienced community practice over the past thirty years, I challenge all residents and academic physicians to experience private practice. Try it if you haven't yet. It is a different world, and you may come to see medicine in a different light from the way you see it now.

DESIGNING A WELCOMING OFFICE

I eventually named my office Sok-comfort Clinic. In Korean, sok means inside, referring to the body or one's mind. It also implies the abdomen or belly, including all the digestive organs. The name was perfect for a gastrointestinal clinic.

After about ten years of practice, I purchased a small building in Englewood, New Jersey, which became my primary office. The building was originally a car dealership. It was run-down, requiring major construction. The entire interior was gutted and rebuilt. The office was conveniently located on the ground floor with a parking lot in front, allowing easy access even for handicapped patients. With Miki's invaluable architectural expertise, we designed a workable office. Despite a lot of work, we had a great time building a new home for our patients.

On the first floor, we had a waiting room, nurses' workstation, patient consultation room, examining room, endoscopy suite, recovery room, and endoscope washroom. The second floor had a locker room, lunchroom, and two additional office spaces. We designed a large bathroom to accommodate patients and another bathroom for staff. In addition, there were other rooms for storage and computer servers.

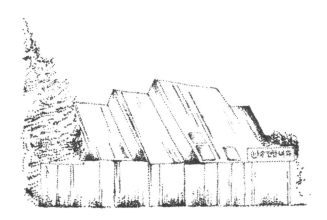

A doctor's office is where patients initially come to consult and address their issues. It's the first place where patients meet their doctors. Providing a safe and comfortable space where patients could feel welcome and greeted was essential. We also wanted an office that had the latest advanced medical technology.

Before starting interviews and exams, providers must carefully observe their patients, especially their facial expressions. To ensure a welcoming environment, I instructed my staff to greet each patient with warm eye contact and genuine smiles.

Miki and I both recognized the significance of the reception area. We located the reception entrance in front of the reception desk, leading to the waiting room. Miki designed the reception area with tall ceilings that created a feeling of a spacious hall. Windows on one side provided patients with a view outside. We put small tables and chairs near the windows to create a café-like atmosphere. A fireplace on the other side of the reception area provided patients with warmth during the colder months, and watching the fire eased their stress and anxiety. Another critical area in a medical practice is the space where nurses, receptionists, and physicians can work together efficiently. Miki and I divided the nursing area into three parts: a private corner for phlebotomy, a semi-open conference area to accommodate patients and their family members, and workstations with computers and telephones.

It was important to us to be able to move from one room to another with ease and efficiency. Therefore, we had to consider how these rooms connected to make sense and create a safe and efficient environment.

We tried to infuse a more welcoming approach to medicine. Even with the advantages of advanced science and technology, clinical staff members cannot maximize their potential without genuine heart and passion—the human elements that science and technology lack. For example, uplifting music paired with beautiful flowers in the waiting room can empower patients, creating an ambiance of cheer and hope. Likewise, clinicians' empathy toward their patients must be palpable, and these efforts to develop open, serene environments are critical components of clinical care.

PATIENT EDUCATION AND ADVOCACY

"Can you tell me what is wrong with me?" my patients continue to ask. How frustrating and anxiety-provoking would it be for patients who consult two to three doctors for answers about their illness and still are unsuccessful in getting a response? Many patients complain that doctors do not explain enough. I have heard numerous complaints that doctors spend most of their time with patients looking at a computer monitor. I remember one patient telling me that her doctor looked at her face for less than one minute during her fifteen-minute visit. He was busy staring at the computer screen.

Communication is crucial for understanding patients' problems. But for the Korean American population, the problem with communication lies in linguistic and cultural barriers. Actually, these problems are not limited to immigrants who do not speak English fluently. The American public has varying levels of health literacy, revealing the importance of health education and communication. Significant variations in diseases exist among ethnicities, and providers must understand this fact and treat their patients accordingly. The American health-care system must formally recognize and accommodate these health disparities.

WRITING TO PROMOTE HEALTH LITERACY

I wanted my medical career to include providing patients with up-to-date health information. Unfortunately, health literacy often does not directly correlate with general literacy. I found this to be especially true in the immigrant population. Many of my patients are well educated, but they are often unaware of essential health information. Given the cultural and linguistic factors, they need help to access important information in a foreign country. To address this issue, I published a health newsletter in Korean. My newsletter contained a wide range of clinical information. It included health news, tips on recognizing symptoms and signs of gastrointestinal diseases, basic insurance coverage details, and articles on US health care. The nurses in my practice also pitched in and wrote short columns on simple but essential health topics.

In 1998, I also started writing a weekly health column in Korean newspapers distributed in New York and other major US cities. The purpose of my column was twofold: to provide the public with the necessary knowledge about various digestive disorders and to help readers understand the health-care system in the US so they could be proficient in accessing care. These writing activities gradually evolved into my book, *Six Steps Toward Digestive Well-Being*, published in 2005 in Seoul.

I wrote my second book, *Chronic Hepatitis B: Diagnosis and Management*. Those two books were first published in Korea in 2008, followed by second and third editions in 2010 and 2014. The second book discussed the treatment, diagnosis, and management of viral hepatitis B, including up-to-date information on antiviral therapy. The idea for this book came about when I visited Korea in early 2008. While I was roaming around checking out mega-bookstores in Gangnam, Seoul, I noticed there were only a few books on chronic hepatitis B for the lay audience. I found this shocking because liver diseases are among the top illnesses that kill Koreans. The hepatitis B virus was the predominant cause of liver disease. In the United States, hepatitis B is also one of the major causes of liver-related morbidity and mortality among Asian Americans. Although health insurance covers hepatitis B screening now, many primary care physicians still do not screen Asian individuals who may be at risk for hepatitis B. There is a serious demand for public education on hepatitis B.

While writing these books, I noticed a significant change in my life. By focusing on my patients' perspectives, I gained a better understanding of the issues and frustrations they experience. The goal of my books was to be informative to my readers, but I also greatly benefited by writing them. They were transforming experiences. Writing gave me the ownership and motivation to improve patient care. It helped me recognize the significance of cultural competence in health care. The US is a country of various ethnicities and races, yet its health-care system does not accommodate the needs arising from this diversity.

CAMPAIGN AGAINST HEPATITIS B

I became involved in a variety of community health campaigns. In 2007, I joined the Asian Health Services at Holy Name Medical Center in Teaneck, New Jersey. In addition, I created the Asian Liver Center at the same hospital to start a hepatitis B diagnosis and treatment campaign. I designed the campaign to reach out to Asian Americans and address their health issues in a way that overcame cultural and language barriers.

Hepatitis B remains a significant public health issue affecting millions of people in the US and more than 250 million globally, but it is under-recognized and under-addressed. There is a severe need for continued prevention, control, and management of HBV care in the US. We need more than screening and vaccination. We must implement a wide range of public health interventions such as education, community empowerment and engagement, and collaborative partnerships with sensitivity to sociocultural determinants of health.

I have worked with vulnerable Asian and African immigrants who suffer disproportionately high rates of hepatitis B infections. Unfortunately, many members of this population have severe complications and end-stage liver disease. I specifically remember a fifty-nine-year-old Chinese American patient who had lived in the United States for fourteen years as a naturalized citizen. She knew she had been chronically infected with hepatitis B for years. She felt well and had no symptoms but knew she needed a liver cancer screening, so she went to a doctor. Unfortunately, she told me that each visit was disappointing due to language and cultural barriers.

At a follow-up visit to my office, a liver sonogram revealed a large mass in her liver, later confirmed as a malignancy. I didn't know how to break the news, but I said, "The sonogram result is not good, but there may be something we can do." I saw the massive disappointment and sadness on her face.

"What do you see? Do I have cancer?" she asked anxiously.

"Well, the sonogram shows a mass in your liver," I responded gently. "Given your recent blood test result, this is likely liver cancer." I assured her that I would refer her to one of the best liver surgeons in the city.

"You need more tests," I said. "Although the mass is not small, it may be in a favorable location for surgery."

I felt very frustrated, having seen a number of similar cases over the years. If this patient had been screened for liver cancer earlier, she might have been able to avoid a late diagnosis. Had there been enough educational campaigns about screening for liver cancer in patients with hepatitis B, similar to the colon cancer screening campaigns in the US, her cancer could have been detected much earlier. It was also possible that her cancer could have been prevented if she had received antiviral therapy for her hepatitis B at an early stage.

Linguistic and cultural barriers still exist even after immigrants have lived in the US for decades. Hospitals must realize that having an interpreter alone does not make the medical service culturally competent or effective. Doctors, policymakers, and policy administrators are all responsible for the disparity and lack of access to care.

Eventually, I founded a nonprofit organization named the Center for Viral Hepatitis with a mission to raise awareness of viral hepatitis in immigrant communities. I was able to get community education grants from a variety of nonprofit organizations. I used these funds to support hepatitis B diagnosis and treatment campaigns at Holy Name Medical Center, Englewood Hospital, and other community organizations. Subsequently, I published articles in peer-reviewed journals, reporting on the prevalence and care of hepatitis B in Asian American communities.

CAMPAIGN AGAINST STOMACH CANCER

Stomach cancer is another disease in which we see racial and ethnic disparities in the US, with Korean Americans experiencing the worst impact. In 2018, I helped organize the Asian American Stomach Cancer Task Force. Although stomach cancer is the third leading cause of cancer deaths worldwide, the overall incidence of gastric cancer in the United States is low, which is why there is no national guideline for screening for stomach cancer in the US. Stomach cancer incidence varies substantially by race and ethnicity, with Korean Americans experiencing the highest rate. In addition, there is a striking disparity in stomach cancer mortality between Korean Americans and Koreans living in Korea. The mortality rate of Koreans in Korea is significantly lower than that of Korean Americans. These findings warrant preventative strategies for the affected ethnic groups in the US.

The task force aimed to raise awareness of stomach cancer in both the public and the US government and initiate screening for high-risk populations. We also planned to collaborate with community organizations and hospitals to provide linkage to clinical care so the available treatment becomes more accessible, especially to those who are disadvantaged.

We live in a racially and ethnically diverse world. Health care must be tailored to meet patients' social, cultural, and linguistic needs. Cultural determinants of health encompass one's beliefs, practices, and values that influence health. We must include these components in a holistic approach and build considerations for minority health into the US health-care infrastructure. For example, the high incidence of stomach cancer and chronic hepatitis B among Asians is an issue that often gets overlooked. The health issues faced by minorities are not considered major "public health" concerns by the US government. This is due to a lack of political will and funding. Interventions will not be implemented without political and societal support.

ETHNICALLY DIVERSE DOCTORS

The United States has a uniquely diverse population, offering a wealth of human resources. According to the 2018 Association of American Medical Colleges diversity data on medical education and the physician workforce, 56 percent of active physicians are non-Hispanic Whites, 17 percent Asians, 6 percent Hispanics, 5 percent African Americans, and 14 percent of unknown ethnicity. Approximately a quarter of these physicians are international medical graduates (IMGs), which refers to those who went to medical schools outside the United States.

Because there are not enough medical doctors in the US, IMGs have always played a vital role in US health care. While most IMGs have been foreign-born non-US citizens, this is no longer the case in recent decades. In the 2020 residency match (a system through which medical students get placed into residency programs), 12,074 IMGs applied for US residency positions. Of these, 5,167 IMGs (42.7 percent) were US citizens, demonstrating that a growing percentage of US doctors are IMGs. The number of IMGs in practice has grown by nearly 18 percent since 2010. IMGs have the most prominent presence in geriatric medicine in the US, accounting for 3,097 out of 5,974 (52 percent) of geriatric doctors. These numbers illustrate the vital role of ethnic diversity among physicians in the US physician workforce.

Given these data on ethnic diversity and expected growth in the immigrant population, ethnic physician organizations play a vital role in US health care. There are about sixty ethnic physician organizations in the US, with varying missions and membership numbers. While some focus on raising awareness and promoting health care in their respective communities, others aim to connect physicians of similar heritages who contribute to health care overall. The Korean American Medical Association (KAMA) is one such organization established as a not-for-profit US physician organization with a vision to empower physicians of Korean heritage and positively impact the health aspects of the US and global community.

KAMA: A MODEL FOR ETHNIC MEDICAL ORGANIZATIONS

In 2008, I became an active KAMA member. After serving as the chair of KAMA's annual scientific program in 2009, I became its president in 2011 and worked diligently to create a nationwide platform for Korean American physicians.

Decades after KAMA's founding in 1974, its membership experienced a shift from first-generation immigrants to US-born, second-generation physicians. This shift brought about varying perceptions of Korean American identity among its members, leading to questions and skepticism concerning the organizational identity and vision. There were also questions and disagreements on organizational structure, culture, and leadership issues.

These challenges are not unique to KAMA and may be common problems faced by every ethnic physician organization. The American Association of Physicians of Indian Origin (AAPI), founded in 1982, is a good example. Just like KAMA, AAPI represents the values and interests of thousands of physicians of Indian origin in the US. AAPI sought to provide a platform for medical students, residents, and fellows of Indian heritage. Similarly, there are US organizations serving the interests of Chinese, Filipino, and numerous other ethnic American physicians. Analyzing the challenging issues in KAMA might provide helpful insights for other ethnic American organizations.

Ethnic identity overlaps with racial, cultural, and national identities. Second-generation physicians who have adopted American culture espouse an identity distinct from their parents. Additional differences between first and second generations include their attitudes and perspectives toward social values and their experiences in the US. These differences in identity and personal outlooks could affect individuals' engagement in their community.

KAMA has a mixed identity, which makes it challenging to unite and function efficiently. For KAMA to thrive, we need a firm organizational culture, which could help integrate the group to make plans and execute activities. In addition, leadership with solid core values and a culture that can guide younger generations is a must. Leadership can create and modify culture, but culture can also define leadership. We must be adaptable and flexible, ready to learn new things, and promote a culture of honesty and empathy. My experiences taught me that KAMA needs something beyond ethnic identity to shape its organizational identity, vision, and goals that resonate with young generations.

PUBLIC HEALTH: A MULTIDISCIPLINARY APPROACH

In my formal education and postgraduate training, I don't remember taking a course discussing the roles of nonbiomedical factors in medicine or health outcomes. It wasn't until I was in private practice for ten years that I realized the critical functions of socioeconomic and cultural factors in medicine, along with the roles of politics and social policies that are at play. Looking back, I see how blind and naïve I was throughout my training at all the institutions, regardless of how excellent they were.

Doctors can't do it alone. In addition to scientists, engineers, and hospital administrators, we need sociologists, public health experts, and policymakers to tackle today's problems in health care. Health care is now a dynamic multidisciplinary field in which medicine and other nonmedical and nonscientific fields must collaborate.

I wanted to seek out how physicians can be instrumental in bringing new avenues of collaboration to improve population health, so I became interested in studying public health. Public health studies how sociocultural and environmental contexts affect patients' disease processes, which modern advanced medical science and technology often ignore. I also became interested in learning about new public-health issues that complement my background and interests in community health, so I enrolled in the Executive MPH Program at Columbia University's Mailman School of Public Health in 2019. I had just turned sixty-five and was receiving Medicare.

I thought about why I wanted to return to school at this point in my career. I have seen people who pursue education at later ages. Some haven't had a chance to finish their college education, and it was their life goal to finish college. I also knew of one retired physician who had a late calling, or rather, he found a new passion. He went to law school and is now practicing law. It's never too late. It's not that I have no degrees, and I am not a degree-seeker.

Aside from many good reasons for anyone to enroll in a public health school, I wondered about preparing for another stage of my life that precedes old age. That's right. Some people may call it the second stage of adulthood in the life cycle. Most physicians my age consider retiring, but the meaning of "retirement" has already changed. Perhaps baby boomers have played a leading role in redefining retirement. Thanks to the good health and longevity enjoyed today, many of retirement age are still working and even looking for new careers. With ample experience and expertise, these retirement-age people have much to contribute to improving the future of our society. Not only have they learned from their mistakes and rich experience from the past, but they also have the maturity, commitment, and strong free will to contribute, and hopefully, the wisdom to be innovative in altering the shape of public life in America. Retirement age is not too late to do more or something different. The doorway to this new stage of life is thinking differently and continuing to learn. The years after age sixty-five should not be seen as a time to sit back and relax. Instead, these years can be a time for creativity and meaningful engagement if that is what makes you happy. After all, we are the ones who have the experience. We also have learned to adapt through good times and bad. Who else can be better qualified to engage the future?

I wondered at the time if tackling this challenge was because of my resistance to old age or the inevitable stage of inactivity in the future. Was it my selfishness, seeking the recognition that shows I can still achieve? Was it personal greed or my devotion? Honestly, I could not discount the greed component. But I realized that I identify with the work I had devoted the past thirty years to: patient care, medical writing, and community health education and research. Continuing to work to engage with these issues and be creative is essential to my life. Going to school was one way to keep me happy.

No matter how well I can justify going back to school, not that it needs any justification, it was awkward to return to school after a long hiatus. But I quickly adjusted to it. Although I spent nearly three decades in private practice, I have always been close to academia. Public health was not alien to me because I was already involved in community health, conducting health disparity research, and actively publishing in peer-reviewed journals. Returning to school was another *step* toward reevaluating medicine and health care from a different perspective. It also offered me a pause to look back at how I had been living my life and allowed me to readjust my future direction.

It was purely coincidental that my daughter and I both enrolled in the master's in public health program at Columbia. Sarah had just graduated from Lehigh University, majoring in anthropology. She was contemplating whether medicine was the right career, so she wanted to pursue an MPH. Her MPH program was a regular one, whereas mine was an executive program designed for physicians and other professionals in health care.

At the time we were in school together, Sarah lived in an apartment on 161st Street and Broadway, so I didn't get to see her often enough. One Thursday morning, I was sitting in the library reading room on the first floor of the Hammer Health Sciences Building. I texted her, "How are you doing, Sarah? I am heading to my epidemiology class.

Do you want to have lunch with me later?"

She replied instantly, "Hi, Dad. I am good. Maybe next time. I have a group meeting over lunch today."

Some classmates teased me that I got turned down by my daughter. I might have tried another time, but I never had that lunch with Sarah on campus. Sarah might have felt uneasy about letting her classmates know her dad was simultaneously in the same MPH school. She was perhaps too shy. But as our MPH programs were of different makeups, we never ran into each other. There were many times, though, when Sarah and I texted each other in school. We would often be studying on different floors of the same building.

Although we never attended the same class, I will always cherish the fact that I was back at school with my daughter at the same school. I am unsure how Sarah will feel many years from now about me returning to school and being in the same degree program as her. One thing I know for sure is that this will be a substantial memory in her life.

My family and friends initially thought I was crazy to return to school. Was I such an oddball? I soon realized that I was not alone. About half of my classmates were physicians with varying degrees of experience, and the other half were professionals from different backgrounds, including law, pharmaceutical corporations, finance, government, and other health-care enterprises. Although more than several looked to be in their fifties and above, the average class age was around forty. It didn't take long to realize that I was the oldest in the class, but I am not sure if the class knew that. However, no matter how old you are and what you might have achieved in your past life, learning can always bring new personal and professional perspectives. In searching for those unique perspectives, we often want to change our lives to find new passions and improve our lives. While I felt this way, some of my younger classmates might not have felt that way. As all the students were professionals who were working full time elsewhere, they enrolled in the MPH program to advance their careers. For instance, some wanted to become a director to advance from their current associate directorship, and others wanted to move into the health-care industry.

One day at the beginning of school, I accidentally overheard a conversation my classmates were having over lunch. They were talking about how many years it had been since they last attended classes. One of the youngest, a dentist in his mid-thirties, said, "It's been years since I attended regular classes like this. I am so tired of school, but I need this program. But you know, when I become sixty, that's it, man. I will be done. I will retire and go someplace and enjoy my life." Of course, he wasn't saying this so I could hear him. I didn't mind him saying that, because he was not much off from what my friends used to say. But I wondered what he would think about what he said when he became over sixty himself.

Besides being digitally fluent, most of my millennial classmates were vocal about the injustices of social and racial inequities—diversity matters regarding gender, race, and identity. I thoroughly enjoyed being in the company of younger professionals, feeling their energy and bold outlooks on life. It could be that young mindset I was seeking, and school was one great place to find and cultivate it.

I spent four full days in class every month for twenty-four months. The workload was hefty and required plenty of reading and writing. The courses covered organizational leadership and management, health policy and public health, and health systems. I appreciated that most of these courses included political and legal perspectives. The program prompted me to reflect on my experiences as a practitioner and what we may anticipate in the decades ahead. I developed insights into many current issues, including the future of Medicare and Medicaid, potential solutions to the rising cost of health care, corporatization of health care, and many more.

One main course that struck me was Managerial and Organizational Behavior. It addressed many complex issues of the current health-care system, such as communication, diversity, group dynamics, teamwork, and conflict management. While the course led me to see the increasing complexity of current health-care systems, it also taught me how good leadership can successfully help navigate the rapid changes in today's health care. It also helped me reflect on my own experiences as a physician. The program was an eye-opener to the reality of my practice and what we may see in the future.

The learning was interactive, and the program provided collaborative learning and case studies resembling the real-world workplace. Students spoke from their perspectives and experiences in the pharma industry, hospital administration, insurance management, and more. I learned so much from others. It was time to free myself to see things from other points of view. It was time to push myself to think outside the box.

VII.
FAMILY,
CULTURE,
AND
IDENTITY

WELCOMING OUR BABY DAUGHTER

After we got married, Miki and I moved around quite a bit, leading hectic lives. Finally, about eight years after our wedding, we were ready to be parents. We tried, but it wasn't easy. Another seven years passed, and finally Miki got pregnant. It was a miraculous thing. Our daughter Sarah came to us precisely fifteen years after our wedding. Thank you, Sarah, for making me a dad.

But, to tell the truth, it was not easy. Easy? Of course, it wasn't. Speaking of hard times, it is interesting that I usually *don't* seem to remember much about the struggles. Perhaps I have been fortunate most of my life. But at the same time, I am the type of person who tends to forget the problematic aspects. Perhaps I try to program my brain to force me to forget bad memories. One hard time—perhaps my most significant struggle—was when Miki and I were trying to have a baby and it didn't work. We had been married for eight years. Miki was thirty-one, and I was thirty-six. We tried all kinds of methods, including intrauterine insemination and in vitro fertilization, but they didn't work. It took another seven years before Miki became pregnant. I still call it a miracle. Those years of waiting were tough.

My concern was mainly about Miki. I would have been willing to adopt a baby if we couldn't have one naturally. Sometimes things don't work out no matter what you do. We began accepting the limitation. That was okay with me. But I felt it was important for her to go through the process of pregnancy, as it would be a valuable physiological experience for her.

It was New Year's Eve in 1996 when we found out Miki was

pregnant. We were sitting in our living room having tea after dinner when Miki approached me. She looked at me, half-smiling. "Chul, I have something to tell you ... I may be pregnant!"

I couldn't believe what I had just heard. "What? Really? Pregnant? Are you sure?"

She said, "Yes, I think so. I missed my last period. I just did a home pregnancy test, and I think it is positive!" And she showed me the two stripes on the test strip.

Yes, it was *two* stripes, alright! I looked at it again and again, doubting what I was seeing. While we were overjoyed and excited, we wanted to have this confirmed.

"Let's go and see Dr. Berliner tomorrow!" I said.

It was hard to believe, and I was so delighted. *Wow, we are going to have a baby. I am going to be a dad!* How long we had waited for this moment. How hard we had prayed. Now we had nine long months to go. Then Miki and I saw our baby for the first time on the sonogram image. Her first photo shoot! After we found out she was a girl, we named her Sarah. Sarah's Korean name is Seul-Ah, meaning wise (Seul) and beautiful (Ah). We wanted her to live her life with those characteristics.

As I saw Miki's middle expanding, I would lovingly touch her belly. It gave me a deep sense of connecting with my daughter. Later in pregnancy, Sarah would kick, and when Miki felt it, I could also feel the tiny kick. I couldn't wait to meet and hold Sarah in my arms. Miki was thirty-seven then; it was a high-risk pregnancy. Thankfully, Miki has been in good health all along and could carry the pregnancy to full term.

September 6, 1997, precisely at noon, Sarah was born. It was a Saturday, and I was working in my New Jersey office. We knew it would be either that day or the next. The day before Sarah was born, Miki complained of indigestion and felt some pain in her belly. The following day, Miki called her doctor and made an appointment as I headed toward my office. My father-in-law would drive Miki to see Dr. Berliner. While working, I couldn't stop wondering if the baby would be born that day. I was so anxious and nervous.

At last, I received a call from Dr. Berliner at eleven saying, "Chul, she's ready! Where are you?"

I quickly asked, "How close?"

He replied, "Any time now!"

So I announced to my patients in the waiting room that I was becoming a father. They responded with big smiles, saying, "Congratulations! Please go!"

I ran out of my office in New Jersey and rushed toward Winthrop University Hospital. The drive usually took forty-five minutes, but I arrived in thirty minutes! Miki and her parents were waiting in the birthing room. The birthing room had a large living area and could accommodate four to five family members. It was less than one hour since Miki had been admitted, and she was about to begin the birthing process. I told Miki not to worry and assured her everything would go well. I tried to comfort her, but it was hard to shake my anxiety. Around 11:40 a.m., Miki's contractions started. Exactly twenty minutes later, Sarah was born. It was the Year of the Ox.

Looking back, I still find it amazing that Miki spent so little time in labor. I know she had a hard time going through what she went through, but the length of labor was nothing like what she and I had heard of. She actually hadn't even received any analgesic, and everything went smoothly. I remember Dr. Berliner saying, "Miki, you are the type of lady who could bear ten children."

Sarah's grandparents were delighted, saying, "Just like an ox, Sarah will be strong and diligent." A healthy baby was born, and we were grateful. I first noticed Sarah's black hair as Dr. Berliner and I received her.

When Sarah's skin touched my hand, it was an electrifying moment. I couldn't believe it. As if the world was too bright, Sarah closed her eyes tight, and I heard her first cry. Her cry signified the beginning of another world for our family. After cutting the umbilical cord, we carefully looked at Sarah's face and body. She was so beautiful. I hugged Miki and Sarah and said, "Well done! Great job! Thank you, God."

So Miki became a mom, and I became a dad. It was about two years after my father passed away. If he had seen Sarah, how crazy would he have been about her? We had no daughters in our family, so I could imagine him going wild over our new addition.

HOMEBUILDER MIKI

My New Jersey office got very busy, and the commute from our house on Long Island was getting more complex. I wanted to live closer to at least one of my offices, so we decided to move. We found a house in the Palisades, New York, about twenty minutes from my office.

It was an older house, but Miki and I thought we could have it demolished and build a new one. Miki started designing and drawing, planning to build the new house. Exactly two years after that, we moved into our new home. It was August 2001. Our new town of Snedens Landing was the very first village facing the Hudson River north of the George Washington Bridge. Although it is only eleven miles from the George Washington Bridge, it is a beautiful, historic village filled with woods and nature. This new house was the third one built by Miki after our previous homes in Roslyn, Long Island, and another in Hamden, Connecticut. It was such a pleasure and a rewarding experience to have been able to design the space in which we live.

There are many things required to design a house, and we considered three. First, we needed a good location. It is indeed about location, location, location. Second, we had to decide what type of building we wanted to erect. And finally, we considered the compatibility of the design with other houses in the neighborhood.

Snedens Landing is an old village founded in the early 1700s that consists of about seventy residences. This location is famous for George Washington and his men spending time in the area during the late eighteenth century. Because this area is close to the Hudson River, with a narrow width, General Washington used it as a strategic point to attack the British navy passing along the Hudson River.

Because Snedens Landing was a famous historic area in the state, building anything there was challenging. We had to get approvals from the town's Historic Board. Miki considered the area's history, studied existing homes and architecture, and decided to build a colonial-style farmhouse. Unfortunately, our proposal was rejected initially because the board thought the house was too large and a little too contemporary. So we reduced the size of the house and altered one flat part of the roof, and the board passed our proposal.

While many neighbors welcomed the design and our family, some appeared cautious. At any rate, after we received the board's approval, we started construction. I don't know much about architecture, but this experience allowed me to learn about the steps and requirements for building a house, at least a little bit. First, it had to be safe while aesthetically pleasing externally. But just as important, Miki had to design the interior space for practical living. Money was also a factor. A good architect has to consider all these elements, so Miki had to keep them all in mind in designing our new home.

A complete drawing on paper is only the beginning of the construction process. Generally, when architects finish their design, they refer it to a construction company, with a general contractor usually orchestrating all building matters. But we handled it differently. Even after Miki finished the design, she took on the role of general contractor and hired subcontractors to carry out the construction. She picked out and purchased all the materials. She hired carpenters, electricians, plumbers, HVAC experts, tile experts, and maybe ten other specialists, orchestrating all the work. If you've ever built a new house, you know the process can be quite bumpy and difficult at times. There can be accidents, and workers may not always finish their jobs according to plan.

Miki and I carefully considered the house's interior, including the main bedroom, Sarah's room, guest rooms, rooms for our parents, a gym, the kitchen, a family room, and a living room. Purposefully, we did not put doors between the living, dining, and family rooms. Instead, we wanted these spaces to flow into each other as we found this more practical and welcoming.

We designed the living room and kitchen to be large and practical for many hosting activities, such as family gatherings and parties with church members. We considered that this would not be a house for the three of us but an inclusive space for everyone who visited us. In our living room with a high ceiling, we placed a grand piano with enough space to accommodate more than fifty people. We intended to open the living room space, but at the same time, we wanted it to exude coziness. We made the interior design simple, mirroring nature. Our house had many large windows, but we did not adorn them with complex window dressings. Miki selected plain molding that framed the windows, with simple blinds and nothing more. While it might have looked bare, it provided an openness allowing us to enjoy the beautiful nature outside. We wanted the windows to frame the outdoor scenery. More decoration would have obstructed this connection.

As we designed these spaces, we considered our past experiences and envisioned our future lifestyle, resulting in some modifications to the design. It provided us with hope and a vision for our future life. When all construction finally ended, we moved into the house. It was one month before Sarah turned four. What a gratifying experience to move into a place we had designed and built *especially* for ourselves.

MIRRORS TO MY HAPPINESS

Miki and I met at the University of Rochester, and our relationship gradually evolved into marriage. As we did back then, we still call each other Chul and Miki. In Korean tradition, couples call each other "yeobo," meaning "honey." But even after we both turned sixty, I feel awkward calling her yeobo.

After getting married, we moved to quite a few cities for school and work. Although there were many hardships, they were outweighed by the abundant moments of joy and happiness. Through our journey, Miki and I supported each other's dreams. Miki knew I always wanted to become a physician, but I had no idea that Miki would become an architect. I knew nothing about architecture before, but after watching her work for all those years, I learned a lot. As I witnessed Miki dealing with construction specialists from New Haven to Long Island to the Palisades, I participated as her assistant. While I did not help with the design of our new home, I shared my ideas and constructive criticism. "Why is this room so small?" and "I think you should have larger windows in the library," were examples of my contributions.

Throughout our experiences of building and remodeling, our fondness for and attachment to our homes deepened. These houses were not mere buildings but integral parts of our family's life and history. During times of joy and sorrow, our homes always provided a safe haven. For the three of us and our visitors, our homes were special and welcoming places. We have created countless cherished memories within these walls.

During the past twenty years, we have had an abundance of gatherings in our homes, both private and public. We hosted church events, concerts, lectures, fundraisers, and campaigns. Our houses became a place for meeting with others. And the relationships we developed have brought another opportunity, called "mannam," meaning "meeting" or "encounter" in Korean. These relationships generated new mannams and showed us that putting our forces together can produce productive and beautiful lives. We learned that if people get together and put their minds and hearts together, they can accomplish wonderful things together.

At the end of each day, Miki and I usually share what happened during our day. I talk about one or two things in my office, and Miki shares her entire day with me. Sometimes her stories are so long that I find them tiring, and I ask her if her tongue hurts. "Can't you just tell me the main points?" I beg of her. Miki talks earnestly about the people she met that day, and the things that took place reflect how much she cares about her work.

"Today, I met a new plumber who was such a nice guy from El Salvador. He has three children ..." and so she continues. It was extremely rare to hear any complaint from her. She puts almost everything in a positive light. Sometimes I want to bring up stories that upset me from my office, but when I hear her cheerful stories, all my negativities hide their tails. *Oh my gosh, how can she be happy all the time? How can she like everything?* I wonder.

During the past five years, we have raised twenty-five chickens producing more than a dozen eggs daily. These eggs are never on our kitchen counter because Miki loves giving eggs out to friends and neighbors. Sometimes, when I search for eggs in my home, I find there are only one or two left. Miki is so friendly to people who come to work at the house. She kindly offers them coffee and lunch, and seeing her happy and generous nature brings joy to me as well.

When I first got to know Miki, I called her "angel." She has an innocent and beautiful heart. Whenever she approaches people, she always smiles brightly. Who would get upset facing someone like that? I don't have the same bright personality. But because of Miki, and since Sarah was born, many positive changes have taken place within me.

I think I'm getting softer and more relaxed. I am happier. Miki and Sarah are the mirrors to my happiness.

JOKBO: ANCESTORS AND IDENTITY

When Sarah was in third grade, she came home with a school assignment asking her to pick one important thing in her house and share it with the class. We started to wonder what to pick out and decided to look around. It dawned on me that when I visited Korea the year before, I had brought home the Hyun family genealogy book (the jokbo)—all nine volumes. I suggested to Sarah that she should show her class our family jokbo.

Since Sarah didn't know what a jokbo was, I had some explaining to do. I explained to Sarah that our jokbo details our entire family's history from 920 AD for over a thousand years, including whom and when each person married, their children, and their occupations. In my family, the oldest recorded ancestor was Hyun Dam-Yoon, who was born in 920 AD. Although there were many ancestors before him, this is our earliest record. I told her that a jokbo is more than a simple family tree. It is an excellent resource on everyday life, culture, and the social history of traditional society.

I am the twenty-ninth generation, and Sarah the thirtieth. After I explained the genealogy book, she looked overwhelmed and seemed to be thinking. Then she asked me, "One thousand years?" Maybe she didn't grasp how vast a span of a thousand years was or how to comprehend this period.

"Yes, Sarah, one thousand years. There are twelve months in a year. Next year, you will be ten years old. Ten times your age at ten is a hundred years old, and ten times a hundred is one thousand years. Do you understand?"

After a pause, Sarah nodded, still looking overwhelmed and surprised. "One-thousand-year record?" she said, looking at the jokbo and clearly awed by its size and significance.

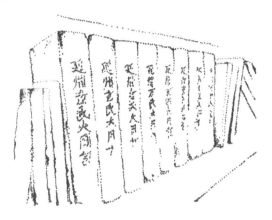

As Sarah and I built a PowerPoint presentation on our family roots, we put the portrait of our first ancestor Hyun Dam-Yoon on the first slide. I explained to her that this great-grandpa Hyun was born in the early 900s, and he was a famous general of the Koryo Dynasty. She asked, "Koryo?" I explained to her that Koryo was named after the ancient Goguryeo Dynasty. And the name Korea was derived from these dynasties.

The first time I faced the Hyun family jokbo was when I was forty. My father suggested I keep a copy of it, but I only opened the jokbo ten years after he passed away and that was out of mere curiosity. I know this is a vital family record, but I was indifferent to it. I was born in Korea, grew up in Asia, and came to the States at nineteen. But, as immigrants, our children are born in the US; many don't speak Korean and are not familiar with the Korean way of life. Understanding their history or a genealogy book would be challenging for these children. But then I wondered, what about children born in Korea? Do they know about their family genealogies? Nowadays, there are web-based genealogies, making it a lot easier to navigate. Yet kids these days do not seem to pay much attention to their family roots.

It is crucial to understand the significance of jokbo rather than merely comprehending the genealogy. I don't expect children to look at the jokbo and understand its contents in detail. The main thing they need to get out of the jokbo, other than who their grandfather is and what he did, is to appreciate the roots of their family and the culture and values built within and through it. Whether it is one thousand years old or one hundred years old, it doesn't matter. What is essential is the understanding of family and its core values. And this becomes a critical factor in validating one's identity in today's ever-diversifying world.

IMMIGRANTS' SEARCH FOR IDENTITY

We often hear and talk about the ethnic identity crisis among second generations in the immigrant population. However, the identity crisis is not limited to the immigrant population. American children may face the same issue if they move to Asia or Africa. By identity crisis, I am referring to uncertainty or confusion about who they are ethno-culturally. Identity may be defined as the combination of traits that differentiate someone from his or her surroundings. When people perceive that they are different from their surroundings, that uniqueness defines them. I know many friends of Asian heritage who came to the US during their childhood and experienced hardships living in this country.

One friend, James, now in his late fifties, came to the US when he was seven years old. His parents immigrated to the US from Taiwan in the early '70s. Hoping their child would receive the best education possible, his parents moved to what James recalls as the whitest neighborhood in Boston, where he was the only Asian kid other than Arun, an Indian student who had also immigrated with his family. Growing up in such a neighborhood, James learned to speak only English. While he was quite well immersed in the White culture, it was impossible to ignore the different way of life at home. Straddling two very different cultures and languages, he grew up trying to adjust. James and Arun were close, because they could identify with each other regarding what they were going through. They were both searching for their place and identity in their adopted country.

I met James during my fellowship. He was one of the medical students rotating through the gastroenterology elective at Yale New Haven Hospital. I never met Arun in person but heard about him through James. Even after his GI rotation, James often visited me during my procedures at the endoscopy suite and later at my laboratory. He didn't have a brother, and I didn't have a younger brother. Soon we became close enough to speak about family matters. One day over lunch, James told me about his girlfriend, Jenny. Jenny was a beautiful girl of Irish and Italian origin.

"Chul, I have been going out with Jenny for over a year. We are thinking about getting married. But I don't know how to break the news to my parents."

Immediately, I knew what was going through his mind. I asked, "Why? Are your parents against interracial marriage?"

He nodded his head and looked helpless. Then he said, "I visited Jenny's parents last week. They both greeted me so warmly. They were already treating me like their son. I wish my parents would do the same for Jenny."

I had seen several similar situations where parents were resistant to their children getting married to someone of a race other than their own. I had no particular advice to offer except to provide assurances. "James, no worries. Take your time, and it will work out," I said.

The United States is often called a melting pot in which various peoples and cultures are melted into a cohesive whole. Indeed, the country has brought in tens of millions and incorporated them into American culture based on broadly shared liberal ideals. But can different cultures contribute their distinct flavors to a new American culture when their cultural practices and values are melted away? Once melted away, all the distinct elements lose their original appearances and unique flavors.

We live in an era of globalization. Increasing connections between nations, peoples, and cultures shape how we live and work with one another. Jokbo reinforces family identity by retaining culture and history. It allows a journey to the past—the past of our ancestors, our family, and where we came from. Our upbringing, professional experiences, and family life are all part of jokbo. It helps us discover our characters and uniqueness, and doing so makes us happy.

DAD, WHAT IS A MINORITY?

Sarah grew up healthy and beautiful. She was quiet and gentle as a child, and we hardly saw her irritated or upset. She was a "problem-free" kid. However, Sarah was cautious and shy when facing people for the first time. She started ballet right before she turned two. One day there was a ballet recital. She wore a beautiful red dress, and when she came out on stage and saw hundreds of people in the audience, she became frightened and ran off stage. The audience laughed. I still remember this quite vividly. However, when she turned three, she was no longer *as* shy, often singing songs and memorizing all the lyrics. We played karaoke and sang together often.

Sarah grew up receiving the love and affection of her grandparents. When she turned four, she entered a pre-K school operated by Columbia's Lamont Institute near our house, followed by kindergarten at Rockland Country Day School in Congers, New York.

When she was around seven, Sarah asked me, "Daddy, what is a minority?"

I was hesitant since this was not normally a question that a seven-year-old asks. She probably heard of minorities from TV news. "Oh, Sarah, a minority is …" I started to explain, unsure if she understood what I was saying, "a smaller group of people compared to a larger group of people. Minority is small, and majority is large. They are opposites. It's like, if you have one hundred oranges and ten apples in a basket, we call the apples the minority and the oranges the majority."

About six months later, Sarah, Miki, and I visited Korea. It was our first trip in twenty years, but it was Sarah's first trip ever. One day, when I took Sarah to the streets of Gangnam, she suddenly pointed her finger at a White person, exclaiming, "There's an American!" She pointed to a tall White man walking down the street. She understood that the people she was used to seeing in New York were seldom seen in the streets of Seoul. At that moment, I recalled when Sarah had asked me what a minority was. I don't think I had given her a satisfactory answer back then. So this time, I gave it another shot.

"Sarah, the number of Koreans in America is minimal, so they are minorities. But here in Korea, the number of White people is minimal, so they are the minorities here. Being a minority is relative and depends on where you are." Sarah looked like she understood, and this made me happy. I told Miki, "I think this alone made visiting Korea worth it."

Sarah finished fourth grade at a public school in Palisades, New York. Afterward, we enrolled her in the Dwight-Englewood School in Englewood, New Jersey. Her school and educational programs in the Palisades were acceptable, but there were very few Asian American students among the predominantly non-Hispanic White American students. We noticed that Dwight-Englewood had a more diverse student population, much like the schools I attended in Taiwan and Okinawa. Miki and I believed this diverse environment would be advantageous for Sarah.

RUNNING: TOOL FOR SURVIVAL

Although I started to run in Okinawa during my high school days, as an adult, I did not continue to run as religiously as I did in my school years. I ran intermittently to keep myself in shape until I restarted in my mid-forties to prepare for a full marathon. It was important to me to prove I could do it before my fiftieth birthday, and I ran my first marathon at age forty-nine. At the time of this writing, I have completed my 115th. Running has guided me and has been a unique energy source.

"Why do you run so much?" "Do you get a runner's high?" "Is there any special reason you started to run?" These are questions I often get asked. People are curious about my obsession with running. Why do I run?

I started running to be fit. As I kept running, I discovered that it helped me reduce stress and improve my mental well-being. It makes me feel less tired and more relaxed, even after long work hours. Of course, if good health is your only objective, you don't need to run marathons. There are plenty of other alternatives. But marathons offer many unique benefits. Training gives me time to enjoy being in nature and time of my own. Marathons let me unwind and be free.

In this busy world, we need time to be alone. Unfortunately, that doesn't happen often. Running provides relief from all the distractions of my daily life and routine. I need time to liberate myself from my work, computers, and iPhones. As I run, I meditate, look back, reflect, and plan for the future. But there are many days I run without any thinking, and this helps me empty my mind. It is a way of recharging.

Marathons also allow for moments to battle with my physical limits. When I overcome these battles, the feelings of achievement are exceptional. Running a marathon is more mental than physical. While running, especially after the twenty-mile mark, my body starts to get exhausted. There is a constant struggle in my mental state whether to slow down and walk or continue to run. It's brain running as well as physical running. It is a fight within me, a mental game. My body is covered in sweat, and my heart pulsates. I feel alive. If you are a runner, you understand what I'm talking about.

BOSTON: A DREAM MARATHON

People often ask me which of the marathon races was the best. It's hard to tell, as each one of them is unique. There are subjective values runners have in favoring one race over others. There are many memorable races. I can include the Boston Marathon on that list. After all, it is one of the four biggest races in the world, along with the New York City, London, and Paris marathons. Every marathoner's dream is to run in Boston, and I was no exception. Unlike the case with most marathons, participants must meet a qualifying time to enter the Boston Marathon. Since I was fifty-six years old in 2010, I had to finish the 26.2 miles before three hours and forty-five minutes. I had worked hard, running six to eight marathons yearly since 2003. Thankfully, I achieved my personal best by finishing in three hours and forty-one minutes in the Mohawk River Marathon in 2010, which qualified me for Boston. I registered to run the Boston Marathon in April 2011. That was two years before the Boston Marathon bombing, a disastrous domestic terrorist attack that occurred on April 15, 2013.

Miki and I drove up to Boston a day before the race. We checked into a hotel near Framingham, which is close to the start area in Hopkinton. The start area was chaotic as thousands of people drove in. However, I felt the energy and anticipation among the runners. Many of these runners were like me, who worked hard to qualify for the Boston Marathon after years of preparation. Having run fifty marathons since 2003, I was excited about taking on this next challenge. I practiced interval training along with long runs to improve my record. Once every other week, I would run about thirty-six miles to develop the stamina to endure the 26.2-mile marathon distance. Interval training consists of repeated rounds of running for a specific interval. For instance, I would run at a slow jogging speed for one minute, followed by high-speed (intensity) running for two minutes, and repeat the same combination throughout the training. Surprisingly, interval training quickened my pace, and I could break the three-hour, forty-five-minute qualifying time.

The cheers during the Boston Marathon were incredible. The roads were narrower than the New York City Marathon, so the noise was deafening when people cheered and screamed. I had never felt such a vibe and energy in any race. A little past the halfway mark, I ran through what people call the Wellesley Scream Tunnel, and the cheering was so loud! Then at about mile twenty, I noted Boston College students were yelling words of encouragement. Finally, I came to the finish a little after four hours. Despite the tired looks and sore legs, I felt a rush of positive energy among the runners. If they were like me, many of them were already thinking about their next race.

ENJOY THE PROCESS

It was an achievement to run the Boston Marathon. So what's next? Of course, it's great to finish the race, but the best part of the marathon takes place before and during the running. The entire process we go through during the race is precious, and we should enjoy it.

I remember a fall race in a small town in upstate New York. At the start, after the national anthem, a local pastor came forward and prayed for a gifted day and the celebration of the race. It was a Sunday morning, and I skipped my regular Sunday services. The pastor prayed, "We often take them for granted, but help us to thank you for giving us these new breaths and the ability to run …" It was such a powerful and heartwarming prayer for me! The course was full of gently rolling hills. Leaves were glowing red in the sunlight, and the warm golden tones under that beautiful autumn sun made me feel alive.

Another race I was impressed with was the run in Prague, in the Czech Republic. The race started in the city's Old Town Square. I left the hotel two miles away and walked toward the start. As I got close to the starting line, I heard music. Soon I realized it was Antonin Dvorak's *New World Symphony*. Its spiritual melody struck me. As I started to run the race, the music continued to play. It was an inspiring moment. The race led me to paths I had never traveled before. Just as in life, it is a journey filled with excitement, aspiration, anxiety, and fear. For me, marathons may be one of the most remarkable ways to experience and celebrate life. Each race we complete marks the start of another one, presenting new challenges to overcome. Throughout these marathons, we feel rejuvenated, experiencing a sense of vitality and vigor. That's why I continue to run; it gives me the energy to carry on with my life.

MARATHON FAMILY ADVENTURES

I have run in thirty-five cities throughout the world. Taking Sarah and Miki along to these cities gave us many memories. We had an RV that added to my enjoyment of traveling to run marathons in the US. When Sarah was six years old, we went to an RV show and spontaneously bought a medium-sized Winnebago RV. We bought this because we wanted to travel and create memories. The RV was a moving condo with a bedroom, bathroom, shower, kitchen, and dining table. Just imagine popping corn and enjoying it while you are being driven in your own vehicle. Sarah's favorite place was a small loft above the driver's seat. We used the RV to attend approximately twenty marathons. We would arrive a day or two before the marathon, parking at an RV park with good views. Then we connected the electricity, plumbing, and sewage. Next, we unpacked, cooked rice, and barbecued. Even eating plain rice tasted good because we were in nature.

ENCOURAGING CULTURAL AWARENESS

I often wondered how American teachers unfamiliar with the Korean language or culture could best teach their Korean students. Even if the students were born in the US, they retain their ethnic and cultural roots. Consequently, their outlook and attitudes would be influenced if not dominated by their parents' or grandparents' way of thinking. This was a question I had for a while. Without knowing the cultural background of their students fully, can a teacher provide a well-rounded education? How effective is education if it is based in the context of predominantly White culture? Wouldn't James and Arun be disadvantaged if their teachers were unfamiliar with Chinese and Indian cultures and histories?

Although our child was born in the US, I believe she is different from American kids. As a result, she is susceptible to developing identity issues. Of course, she may receive the best-quality education, speaking English as fluently as native speakers. But this may not make her happy and free from an identity crisis.

Miki and I gave a lot of thought to Sarah's education, and we participated in the school's PTA and other boards to find ways to be of help to children. Miki became deeply involved in the Sejong Cultural Education Center, where teachers taught the Korean language and culture. Later, we initiated fundraisers to send the Dwight-Englewood School's teachers to Korea along with Sarah and other students. The teachers visited Korea to learn and study Korean culture and experience the history and culture firsthand. Our goal was that this experience would help these teachers understand their Korean students better. The program also benefited Sarah and her Korean American friends as they saw and experienced the roles linguistic and cultural differences can play in education. Although the visits to Korea were only for a few weeks, they provided an excellent opportunity for teachers to understand and learn about Korean culture and, indirectly, their Korean students. Over the course of ten years, we sponsored more than one hundred teachers who were able to apply their newfound knowledge and experiences to their teaching methods.

SARAH'S PATH

We are all concerned about our children's education. Education provides our children and all of us with opportunities to enhance our lives. Education has always been an essential issue in any society. People often take it for granted that parents invest everything in their children's education. In Korea and many other Asian countries, this burning enthusiasm for education is demonstrated when young children are sent to a foreign country in their first and second grades. If my parents hadn't provided me with a supportive learning environment, I would not be where I am today.

Then what can parents do to help their children's education? The answer varies based on each individual set of parents and family circumstances. In the West, there are names like Tiger Mom or Helicopter Mom. In Korea, TV dramas called *Gangnam Mom* and *Sky Castle* reflect parents' aggressiveness toward their children's education.

But if children are restricted or regulated too tightly, how can their minds be free to learn or study? I remember my elementary school days in Korea. Children had to study day and night to enter middle school. They had to enter the best middle school to get into the best high school and then university. Nothing much has changed since those days. Children younger than ten are already studying extremely hard. In the US, I've heard some Korean American parents saying that, as immigrants, they must put their lives on the line to get their children into the best Ivy League colleges. This inflexible, reckless, and blind attitude of parents is not only futile but is also harmful to their children. Many parents think that when children enter the Ivy League, they have "made it," but if they enter, do they always graduate? And what about after graduation? Some think that just getting in is enough instead of focusing on finishing well. But I think it's more important to finish well and to thrive. I hope I did not impose such reckless attitudes on Sarah's educational path.

I've seen intelligent kids who get into good, competitive schools and then do not finish their education. Others may graduate with good grades but seem lost about their future goals, not knowing what to do after college. I've learned about persevering for the long haul through my own experiences in academics and running. I tell young people, "Life's journey is a long-distance race. It's got ups and downs. It takes time!" And I tell them the most crucial element of their education is to find happiness; that is real success.

Sarah entered Lehigh University in Bethlehem, Pennsylvania, in 2015. She told me several times when she was young that she wanted to become a doctor. Was this because she had seen me working as a doctor and it appealed to her? I don't know. Many children of physicians grow up to become physicians. For about ten years, between 2005 and 2015, when I served in various physician networks, I met physicians worldwide. Sarah accompanied me to many conferences where she had the opportunity to see these interactions.

One day, I asked Sarah what kind of doctor she might want to be if she went into medicine. She said she wanted to be an obstetrician, saying it could be enormously rewarding to participate in bringing life into the world. I remember telling Sarah, "There is a big difference between the study and the practice of medicine. I studied medicine as a basic scientist, thinking that science would give solutions to health care. But health care includes so many other nonmedical nuances. It could be helpful to develop broader skills and perspectives about health care before attending medical school."

Sarah was constantly worried that she wouldn't be able to get into medical school because she didn't do well in her science classes. She said, "Dad, I don't think I am good at science. You know my grades in general chemistry and biology. I am worried if I can make it into medical school. And even if I did, would I become a good doctor?"

I replied, "Sarah, Dad did poorly in organic chemistry and a few science courses. But I had no problem in becoming a doctor. Medicine is not only a science; it's more of an art. I know how you did in science classes, and having gone through medical school myself, I can assure you that you will do just fine in medical school."

She might have thought I was trying to make her feel better and encourage her, but I meant what I said. But then, she looked at me, and asked, "Are you sure, Dad?"

I said, "Sarah, you must decide if you want to be a doctor. But don't let that decision be affected by your science grades."

I often wonder if I had unintentionally pressured her to consider medicine. Or she might have felt that is what I wanted. I could have subconsciously conveyed my desire for her future career. Sometimes I was demanding of her academic performance when I felt she needed some pressure. I know I shouldn't have done that, and I hope I didn't do it too much. If I did, however, I hope it will not negatively impact her future. I wish for her to find her own passion and work hard for it.

Sarah majored in anthropology at Lehigh. She developed her talent and passion for medicine through her extracurricular activities. She founded the Medical Anthropology Association at Lehigh, actively participating as its first president and creating forums to encompass science and humanities. Through these activities, she had the opportunity to invite students and professors to create a platform to address multidisciplinary issues.

Unsure about moving into medicine directly after college, Sarah continued her postgraduate education by pursuing a master's degree in public health at Columbia University. An MPH would be an excellent bridge to connect her anthropology background to medicine if she decided to pursue a medical career. Toward the end of her first year, in 2020, the coronavirus pandemic hit and paralyzed all branches of society, causing a human catastrophe with millions of deaths worldwide. At the same time, the pandemic exposed numerous deficiencies we have within the health-care system in the US and globally. It also provided a learning opportunity to reexamine underserved communities' health inequities and rethink our future.

After earning her MPH, Sarah explored her interests in design and architecture. Her decision was rather shocking to me. Initially, I was disappointed, but who am I to judge what is best for her career and life? I said to myself and Miki, "She is still too young. Let her explore, and we will support her however we can!" What she decides to do and how she will live her life remain to be seen. I hope she finds and follows her passion steadily no matter how long it takes and whatever hardships she may encounter, just as we see in the marathon journey.

In 2018, Sarah was a senior at Lehigh. She had come home to visit, and I was driving her back to school when I brought up the story of her grandfather's surprise visit to Johns Hopkins. Sarah had never met her grandfather but remembered his birthday better than I did. She thought of her grandpa as Grandpa Philip, as that was his American name. Between her grandma and myself, she heard many stories that made her feel familiar with him.

If my father was alive, I can't imagine how much he would have adored his only granddaughter. One thing I am sure he would have done with Sarah if he was alive was to take her ice skating as soon as she could walk! I can picture my father enthusiastically waiting for Sarah to take her first steps so he could put her little feet into skates. Then, he would have loved to take her out to buy her dresses and treat her to ice cream. How adorable he would have found my Sarah. He would have devoted all his time to spoiling her!

Did I think of my father because I was traveling to Sarah's school? Or was it because my father's thoughts and love toward me resembled my thoughts and love toward Sarah? At any rate, I started to tell Sarah, "When I was a senior in college, just like you, Grandpa Philip paid a surprise visit to my school. Sarah, it's so strange how I can vividly recall his sudden visit that year. He appeared lonely, and I can now feel an abundance of his love and warmth. He explained why he had come, saying, 'I just came to see you.' I did not know then that those simple words could embrace so much of my dad's love and care toward me."

Sarah listened to me quietly, probably thinking to herself, *Dad, I think you miss him.*

LOSING MOM

My mother passed away a week after Sarah entered college. I was in the middle of doing a procedure at my office when a phone call came from the nursing home. My mother had a hip fracture and had undergone surgery a year before, and as a result, she was not ambulatory and was in a nursing home. The nurse spoke to me, "Your mother stopped breathing."

"What?" I didn't know what to say. I had just spoken to her that morning. "What happened?"

My mother had recently complained of shortness of breath and was seen by various physicians. But they discovered no abnormalities. Six months before, she developed ventricular tachycardia (a dangerously rapid heart rate), which was successfully managed with cardioversion—a medical procedure using electricity or drugs to restore an abnormally fast heart rate or another cardiac arrhythmia to a normal rhythm. Subsequently, she had an automatic defibrillator implanted, and she seemed to be doing well.

The nurse reported that my mom was found unconscious and without a pulse. EMTs came immediately and administered CPR followed by intubation, but they were unable to resuscitate her. What happened? Did she have another severe arrhythmia, causing a deadly impact on her heart? Did the defibrillator malfunction? Did she aspirate? I was very disturbed because I had no answers. How many times have I revisited that moment when Mom was losing her breath? *Ah, I should have been there. But how?*

Although my mom was almost ninety-two, she was mentally sharp as she had always been. Her death was sudden, and wondering what might have gone wrong with her bothered me. She had been anxious about wanting to leave the nursing home. I understood and assured her that returning to her condo would be possible once she finished her rehabilitation from surgery. I was also considering that she should come to live with us. Was her death related to her heart? She had complained of shortness of breath intermittently, which I believed was attributed to her anxiety. Her cardiac checkups after the automatic defibrillator placement were normal. Was there anything else we missed? I felt guilty, thinking I had overlooked something.

Only several days before, I met my mother to plan her ninety-second birthday party, which was coming up in two weeks. We planned to hold the party at our house. We talked about whom she wanted to invite. I asked if there was anything she wanted for her birthday.

My mother was very independent, and she wanted to live on her own. As she aged, she lived in a one-bedroom apartment and shopped and cooked on her own. Unlike my dad, she could engage in conversation with anyone of any age and make them laugh. Her church was an important part of her life, and she was active in church gatherings. And she was a superb cook. I have many fond memories of my mom's cooking. When I came home for breaks from college, she would cook delicious Korean dishes. It was her joy to cook for her son, and I will never forget the excited expression on her face as she prepared food. My mom felt I needed energy after being away from home for months.

Visibly animated, she would say, "Chulsoo-ya, you look tired. Did you lose weight? Of course, the food at the school won't be good enough. What would you like to eat?" She would get all excited and rush to the grocery store. Beyond giving her joy, it was her mission to have her son eat something substantial and good.

One typical dish she prepared for me was gomtang, a traditional Korean meat and soup dish made from bone and beef. It would take about six to eight hours to extract the broth from the bones, creating a nutritious and delicious soup. My favorite was oxtail soup. Once prepared, I would first eat the meat part with homemade soy sauce garnished with scallions, garlic, and hot peppers. After I ate the meat part, I would mix rice in the clear meat broth. Then I would put kimchi on top of the rice and eat that. The meat was so soft and delicious, and the soup was beyond what you could find anywhere else in this world. This mixture of rice, broth, and kimchi created a harmony I will never taste again. I can still recall that smell and taste. It was just heavenly.

When I was ready to return to school after a few days of nourishment, my mom would pack kimbap, just made that morning with the freshest ingredients and wrapped with seaweed. Then, she would say, "This dish is for you, and the other is for your friends at school."

Even in her late eighties, she would make mandoo and kimchi for me and my family. I questioned her about why she didn't want to live with us. Although she was aging, she wanted to remain independent. I didn't fully understand why she wanted to live alone at her age.

My mom passed away twenty years after my dad's passing, and suddenly my shortcomings as a son hit me hard, and I felt very sorry for my mom. She and I had many arguments because we were both very picky and stubborn. We often argued over trifling things, raising our voices. We had different outlooks and perspectives but were similar in many ways, and we both hated to lose. But what could be gained from arguing with my own mom? Why wasn't I warmer or softer? I should have hugged her every time I saw her, but I didn't. I was often too curt, and I hope she forgave me for the times I treated her coldly.

I am grateful for my mother's strong-willed character, which I inherited. Thanks to that kind of character, I persisted in my goals. I owe all these good things and more to my mother.

A few months before her passing, she often said, "I'm so thankful I lived long enough to see Sarah start college." She was happy and excited to see how Sarah grew into a healthy and beautiful young lady. Sarah loved her grandma so much and took great care of her. How could I thank Miki enough, who, since we married, had cared for my mother better than Mom's two sons?

When I returned home to be with my family on the day of Mom's passing, I recalled that Miki started to sing hymns for my father when he was on his deathbed many years before. If anything consoled me, it was that Mom was reunited with my father in heaven. Then, suddenly, I felt overcome and went into a room and sobbed. Sarah followed me into the room and gave me a tight hug.

It has already been eight years since Mom passed away. But strangely, it doesn't feel that long ago. All my memories about her, good and bad, are now beautiful remnants of her. Mom will always live within me as those memories continue to stay so intact in my thoughts.

EPILOGUE

WRITING THIS BOOK PROVIDED ME with a precious opportunity to explore my past. This "tour to the past" was a pleasant one. I relearned who I am and who I have been in different stages of my life. It also helped me reassess my present life and how it connects to my past. When my dad visited me at Johns Hopkins, I was twenty-two years old, and now I have a twenty-six-year-old daughter. This nostalgia about my dad's visit has inspired me to reflect on my past and its impact on who I am. I have come to understand that my past is intertwined with my parents' lives and history, and this has motivated me to learn more about their origins and experiences.

Remembering my dad prompted me to see that I was in the same frame of mind with Sarah as he was with me many years ago. It wasn't until I reached midlife that I fully appreciated the significance of my family culture and identity, and now I am eager to share my insights with Sarah. I have cherished warm relationships with my parents, brother, and now with Miki and Sarah that span generations. Yet, I am only partially capable of understanding the impacts of our family values. The lessons and love that have been passed down through generations are unique and will ensure Sarah and her future generations' well-being throughout their lives.

Immigrants' struggle for identity is challenging, yet crucial. They are living in a situation where they must figure out their place in the world and how they relate to it. This can prompt them to delve into their identities to reconcile their experience of feeling like outsiders. In the process, they learn to retain and nurture their values, traditions, ancestry, and family bonds while also adapting to a new culture.

For Korean Americans, Hallyu (the Korean Wave, which has caused a global catalytic boom in Korean pop culture in music, film, and TV dramas since the '90s) has facilitated our access to our motherland's culture and history. The pride and sense of connection Hallyu can instill in Korean Americans are enormous resources in rediscovering our past and history.

Similarly, the children of immigrants from China, India, and other Asian countries, along with those from Africa and Europe, can derive inspiration from the cultural values of those nations. Indeed, today's world cannot be a melting pot; instead, it is more like kimbap (Korean seaweed rice roll). When rice and other ingredients are wrapped in seaweed, their unique colors, shapes, and flavors are preserved while also contributing to a new and distinct union with a delightful taste.

I also learned that knowing your past alone is not enough to understand your identity. Yes, I wouldn't be who I am without knowing about my past, but how I expanded on and learned from past events also shaped the identity that keeps me going. Our sense of identity isn't static. We change and grow with every new encounter and interaction in different surroundings. Running became an important part of my identity and continues to drive me to discover and express my unique perspectives on life. Running keeps me both physically and mentally in shape. It helps me endure difficult moments. It coaches me in managing my family and professional lives. Running has become a vital part of my identity.

Through this self-exploration of my past, I have found freedom—a powerful force that drives me forward. My strong sense of self-awareness also helps me connect with people in my community and around the world. And it makes me delve deeper than simply recognizing people's ethnic, racial, and cultural differences. I find great joy in being a physician because it gives me the opportunity to meet and get to know people from various backgrounds. I have learned to be more human. This means recognizing that everyone has unique needs and challenges and tailoring my approach to each individual accordingly. I have gained a better understanding of diversity and have become more conscious of the disparities in health care. As a result, I have learned to tailor medical care to meet each person's individual social, cultural, and linguistic needs.

My journey through family interactions, schools, and professional experiences seems endless, like a long race with many ups and downs. It has involved a series of pursuits of an authentic and meaningful life. We all have different life paths and unpredictable futures. But we must learn to never give up and to go forward and live our dreams—the dreams that can bring us confidence and freedom. We should go after the things we feel passionate about, no matter how good or poor we may be at them. Regardless of the hurdles we face, we should try not to despair. Remember, life is a marathon with many surprises. We will not know the outcome of this journey full of discoveries until it comes to an end.

ACKNOWLEDGMENTS

THANKS TO MY DAUGHTER, Sarah, for creating all the illustrations for this book. They bring my story to life and deepen its meaning for me and my readers. When I was looking for an illustrator to portray images from my past, she approached me and asked, "Dad, can I help?" Working with Sarah to craft the illustrations was a unique chance to bolster our bond and reminisce about some of my most cherished memories.

This book is an expression of gratitude to my parents, Miki, Sarah, and my teachers, friends, patients, and university communities in my adopted country. Ultimately, I can't help but thank God for my miraculous journey thus far.

ABOUT THE AUTHOR

CHUL HYUN is a Korean American physician, author, and long-distance runner. He has practiced gastroenterology in New York and New Jersey since 1992. Passionate about health equity, he has founded and served nonprofit community health organizations and published articles on ethnic health disparities in the US. He has published five books on digestive health and is a frequent speaker on various health topics.

Hyun earned his bachelor's degree from Johns Hopkins, PhD in biophysics from the University of Rochester, and MD from the University of Miami, and he completed postdoctoral training at Georgetown, Yale, and the University of Chicago. He recently decided to "shake things up" by earning a master's degree in public health from Columbia University.

An avid runner, Hyun has completed 115 marathons worldwide. Running helps him unwind and feel free. He lives in Palisades, New York, with his wife Miki and daughter Sarah. Visit him online at www. chulhyunauthor.com.

ABOUT THE ILLUSTRATOR

Sarah Hyun is a design and creative consultant with a background in textiles, beauty, and public health. She received her bachelor's degree in anthropology from Lehigh University and her master's degree in public health from Columbia University. Throughout her coursework and free time, she has enjoyed developing her love for illustrating, both traditional and digital. She especially enjoyed collaborating with her dad on this book, her first publication as an illustrator. Sarah looks forward to expanding her artistic reach in future endeavors.

Made in the USA
Middletown, DE
10 October 2023

40407788R00104